T0283818

Praise for *Seaglass*

'These essays investigate the permeable boundaries
between humans and their environment: skin, shore,
water-surface. *Seaglass* is an invitation to live
more fully, think deeply. A true gem.'
Helen Mort

'Kathryn Tann has a poet's eye for fine detail.
These essays are full of intricate, illuminating images,
as bright and surprising as the lozenges of sea glass
Tann searches out on the shore.'
Naomi Booth

'This is a lovely lapidary arrangment of prose fragments and
personal stories. *Seaglass* tells us about skin and swimming;
it delights in dancing and performance and quietly hymns
nature, from pavement weeds to Canadian wilderness.

And much like sea-worn beads of glass garnered
on the shore, the prose here is reflective, refracting and
full of gentle colour, as it leads us to blue pools and
ponders the meditative moments in life.

A book as gentle as the lapping shirr of waves,
as buoyant as the wrap of sun-warmed seawater
around a swimmer's onwards shape.'
Jon Gower

'In *Seaglass*, Kathryn Tann weaves memory, joy in the natural world, and a humble appreciation for those simple acts of communion with bodies of water – being both in and beside them – to create a collection of essays and meditations that are beautifully written and incredibly wise.'
Carly Holmes

'Kathryn Tann sifts through our vast complex and changing world to find the precious moments of stillness and solace that anchor us. Quietly observant, candid and tender, Tann writes movingly about her deep connection to nature, the challenges of growing up and repositioning oneself in the world, and the primal instinct to build a home wherever the tide takes us.'
Karen Powell

'Like the sea glass of her title, Kathryn Tann's essays are a scattering of small bright things – bearing witness to her careful noticings, a grounded probing of the tideswept nature of time, and her faith in curiosity and wonder as guiding lights to navigate our planet's tumultuous changes.'
Linda France

'Kathryn Tann is an exciting new voice, and *Seaglass* is a beautiful collection that shines jewel-like with moments of clear-eyed perception and piercing insight. This book will make you look at the world with fresh eyes.'
Jessica Moor

Seaglass

Seaglass

ESSAYS, MOMENTS
AND REFLECTIONS

Kathryn Tann

2024

Copyright © Kathryn Tann, 2024

All rights reserved. No part of this book may be reproduced in any material form (including photocopying or storing it in any medium by electronic means and whether or not transiently or incidentally to some other use of this publication) without the written permission of the copyright owner. Applications for the copyright owner's written permission to reproduce any part of this publication should be addressed to Calon, University Registry, King Edward VII Avenue, Cardiff CF10 3NS.

www.uwp.co.uk

British Library Cataloguing-in-Publication Data
A catalogue record for this book is available from the British Library.

ISBN: 978-1-915279-62-0

The right of Kathryn Tann to be identified as author of this work has been asserted in accordance with sections 77 and 79 of the Copyright, Designs and Patents Act 1988.

Every effort has been made to contact copyright holders. However, the publisher will be glad to rectify in future editions any inadvertent omissions brought to their attention.

Cover artwork by Jason Anscomb
Typeset by Agnes Graves
Printed by CPI Group (UK) Ltd, Croydon CR0 4YY

The publisher acknowledges the financial support of the Books Council of Wales.

CONTENTS

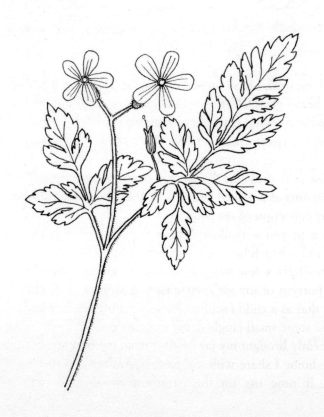

ON COLLECTING
SEA GLASS

For a long time, I have owned a large jar. The jar is made of thick, heavy glass, clear as water, with a beautiful globe for its handle: a crystal marble balanced on the lid. It is just the same as the sweetie jars that lined the walls of the old village shop at St Fagans Museum in Cardiff (the shop that sold the best pear drops in the world). And inside this jar – as mesmerising as a sucked boiled sweet held up to the sunlight – is my collection of sea glass.

I grew up just a stroll away from Penarth seafront. There, the pebbled beach has long been full of human activity, and always offers a few nuggets of smooth glass. I suppose a large portion of my jar's contents comes from there, but I know that as a child I seldom left any rubbly beach without at least some small jangle in my raincoat pocket.

I recently brought my jar of glass from my parents' house to the home I share with my partner, Andrew, on the river Ouse. It now sits on the bathroom windowsill, where the light can illuminate my collection like a stained glass window made with all the seasons' colours of the sea.

Andrew and I get down onto Seaham Hall Beach in County Durham at about midday. Hoods up, zipper pulls pressed to our lips, Velcro flaps closed against a bluster of drizzle and salt spray.

Immediately my eyes are scanning the shingle, and within a yard or two I've spotted one. Bending to pick it up from the other pebbles, I spot another. They are tiny beads – about the size of a rice crispy – but very smooth and round. One green, one reddish brown.

This is old glass, coached in and out for decades by the tide. No pale splinters of pinot grigio bottles here. This glass sits at home among the shingle, wave-worn just like the rock and polished flint. I move along the shore to a band of slightly larger, grape-sized pebbles, hoping to find a similarly weighted piece of treasure. I stoop again for a droplet, the colour of a hot city haze.

The best colours are electric blue, or pale turquoise – the shade of a sand-bedded rock pool in fair weather. It's easy to find beer-brown lumps, and clear pieces made white by the mist of erosion. Your classic bottle green is probably the most frequent find, for obvious reasons. The more unusual tints, like orange, are always exciting. Once, I found a very slim oval of lavender.

There is nothing so disappointing, however, as stooping to pinch a bright new colour of sea glass, only to find that it is a brittle fragment of weightless plastic.

In the late spring of 2020, we were living in a small, rented flat on the second floor of a large apartment block in central Manchester. It was mine and Andrew's first shared home, and we were stuck in it, on account of a national Covid-19 lockdown.

One rainy day, speaking to my dad over the phone, I told him that I'd had enough. 'There's just no wilderness,' I said, 'it's all covered in concrete or spoilt by rubbish, and there's hardly any open space. The park is alright, but it's just mown grass and railings. There's nowhere really *natural* to go to. There's no escape.'

He was standing under a cloudy sky at Barry Docks, at the back of the corrugated warehouse that he works in. He told me that he'd been paying more attention to the weeds. I braced myself, expecting another goose-grass rant.

'No, the flowers!' he said. 'They're actually amazing. Despite everything, despite all this concrete and rubbish, these plants are springing up quite happily. Making this dump much nicer, anyway.' He told me that he'd been coming out here more often, as the weather grew warmer and with no co-workers to talk to. 'There's some real beauty to be found, when you look at it a different way.'

Unconvinced, I told him about the swan nesting on a bed of carrier bags in the old canal behind our building.

'Well, why not? That plastic probably makes a really good nest, well insulated and comfortable.'

'Mmmm. It's not ideal.'

'I know, but try to be optimistic. Nature doesn't care – it's everywhere. It can make the most of what it's got.'

I was surprised by this suggestion, being so used to the usual argument that there's no such thing as wilderness in this well-trodden country. It was everywhere; and of course I knew this. Nature was in the fridge, the carpark, and in the cocktail of bacteria on my palms each time I came home from the supermarket.

A week later, a parcel arrived for us. It was a pair of binoculars from Dad, good ones, just the same as his. We took them out that evening, crossed the bridge over to Salford and followed the river path towards the quays. I tried to ignore the open fridge embedded in the mud, to see the thriving nettles as a sign of nature's industriousness rather than a nasty inconvenience.

We looked for things we could view through the binoculars: geese gliding down the river, up-close seagulls, the usual gangs of mallards. Then, at a tall hedge above the path, shielding a newer block of flats from the grey water down below, we came across a hullabaloo. House sparrows, at least a dozen of them, flitting in and out of the dense leaves, cheeping and chattering to one another. Andrew and I leaned against the railing and passed the binoculars back and fore. I had never paid so much attention to such little birds. They were fascinating.

A young couple jogged by, throwing a quizzical look our way. We stayed, as the sun crept away, for about twenty minutes. It was a busy evening for the sparrows.

After that, in defiance of the constant trickle of bad news coming into our apartment via screens and newspapers, I decided to start collecting – quiet examples of our marks and mess made beautiful, some already known and some newly gathered – a private list of silver linings.

I first found out about Seaham while I was at Durham University. In the midst of multiple essay deadlines, I remember telling two of my friends how I thought the sea might make everything feel a little better. Less than an hour later, five of us were wedged into a Mini Cooper, hurtling towards the nearest beach we'd found on Google Maps. We climbed over fences, crunched across shingle, and finally, we were there: each stood apart on the shore, in our own private spaces, watching the midnight moon spilling out all over the inky sea. But under moonlight the shingle beach was washed of colour – a faded sprawl of shadows: dimples left from the daylight press of many boots.

Today, the ground is technicolour, and every kind of person is stooping to search: parents, toddlers, teenage boys and elderly friends. There are casual glancers: those dog-walkers who can't resist the second take on a possible glint of light. There are the diggers, armed with sand-castle spades, sitting down to focus on one patch. Then there are the professional hunters, welly-booted and hugging the retreating tide, hoping to snatch a newly offered gift from the sea.

I found out recently that jewellery makers come here, to Seaham, from far and wide, combing the beach at first light for free jewels. I don't like it, but I am charmed by the idea of wearing a piece of sea-polished litter – a whisper of the waves around your neck: recycling at its most fashionable. I have been noticing sea glass since I can remember; the only one running to catch up across the sand, slowing a family walk with my foraging. It never occurred to me that these subtle treasures might be an established past-time…let alone a sellable commodity.

Becoming more of a known attraction year on year, the beaches at Seaham are more picked over than ever before. I feel a twitch of selfishness at this, the thought that other people are stealing all of my glass, pocketing the best bits until there's nothing left to find.

But twice a day the stock is resupplied. Glass scoured and rolled underwater for years is finally deposited on land, fresh for new discovery. Of course, there are also special pieces that, if gone unspotted, might be taken back by the waves at the next high tide, never to be offered up again.

At this thought, I search with more vigour than before. As Andrew walks on ahead, I'm unable to tear my gaze from the ground, or even properly converse. I stop and fall behind every few paces, interrupt with gasps of triumph every few sentences. Look at this one. Oh! And this one, this one is even better!

I can see how this kind of treasure hunt might be addictive: searching hungrily for little fragments of light – for the breadcrumbs of by-gone people, sown into the landscape and made beautiful by the elements.

Record no. 1

Behind the terraced warehouses of Barry Docks, a section of forgotten concrete thrives. Late spring blooms in marvellous colours: dog-tongue pink, phone-book yellow, printer-paper white. They don't seem to mind the splayed chairs, the pallets, the broken buckets or rusting joinery. They don't mind at all – are making good use of it, in fact. The bindweed sends its eager tendrils around the rim of a blue plastic barrel, its soft velvet trumpets calling to the sun.

Record no. 2

Just outside the inner ring road in Manchester city centre, a young swan curls herself neatly into her nest, protected by woody buddleia and wall. Graffiti-wrapped archways hold the trains far up and out of sight, thick concrete keeps away the cars, and double-glazing shields her from the Jenga stack of people in their painted white apartments. At night, the glow of the billboard from the road plays the moon; curls of electric light ruffle the surface of the old canal. This narrow channel, forgotten by the city's eyes, is the ideal spot. Yellow wagtails bob along the water's edge.

Later, when the cygnets clamber out from their bed of plastic scraps – a fraying rainbow nest of warmth and careful labour – they will have the perfect place to learn to swim, before they paddle round the old brick bend and into the heavy drift of the Irwell.

Record no. 8

There is an unused track road, crumbled and sprouting, inland along the eastern edge of the Castlemartin Ministry of Defence range in Pembrokeshire. Sunken between two high-hedged banks, each their own complicated ecosystem, it runs downhill and then left into a copse of tangled trees. On the one side, embedded in the overgrown hawthorn, is a tall fence trimmed with barbed-wire coils.

Eventually, this weave of wire and branch is broken by a wide opening and an unlocked gate, ajar enough to slip through onto gravel. The way is marked with enormous boulders: follow them around, around, past the abandoned wetsuit sprawled and bleached under the sun, past the rusted sewing machine and the cracked mosaic mud. And, quite suddenly, there it is: a blue lagoon. An oasis cradled in this unexpected place. A heron flies up from across the lake. A steep shelf drops into the deepest part of the water. Fringing the edges of this quarried bowl, pale young trees – branches wriggling upright, unswept, sheltered from the coastal wind – make the whole scene look like a Mediterranean canyon.

There is a silence, a stillness, a sense of being in a world apart from the farmland up on the cliffs. There are no clues that the crops and cows are up there, just as there was no inkling from the track, the roads, the country lanes, that this crater had been hollowed out of the fields they skirt around.

Record no. 9

Half a mile from the disused quarry, the overgrown access road reaches Bosherston: a cluster of low-gabled houses, a climbers' pub and an ivy-wrapped tearooms. Through the trees, tucked into a groove between village and sea, are the Lily Ponds: a spring-fed network of shallow lakes, circled by footpaths and quiet among the wooded slopes. Worn stone crossings – low walkways or eight-arch bridges – guide the walker through the sheltered valley, and out, with the trickle of the spring water, onto Broad Haven Beach.

The Lily Ponds are not natural; not in the way some might define the term. When the Cawdors of Scotland established their country estate here in the eighteenth century, they stoppered-up the river running out of the gorge, letting water fill its creases, creating their own landscape of tranquillity. It was to be enjoyed by the family during their visits in the summer season. Trees were planted, animals encouraged: a carefully designed transformation on an enormous scale. This sluicing of the fresh springs also made the beach what it is today. What was once a marshy open estuary is now a broad, soft-sanded haven. Over a handful of generations, the dunes have gathered themselves higher and higher, shoring more beauty up against the old Stackpole estate.

Though the grand house is gone, the high view it held over the ponds remains. The woods and waterways are sanctuary to a spectacular variety of species. Lilies unfurl their pink petals in the summer, otters slip under the low water's edge at dawn. The beach itself – cliff-cradled, river running down its side and sands shifting year by year – is my own definition of happiness. As a family, we have syphoned years of joy from its shores. I close my eyes and miss it, often, when I haven't been there for a while.

Record no. 26

Seaham was once home to a glass manufacturer – one of the biggest in Europe. From the 1850s to the 1920s, Londonderry glassworks made up to 20,000 hand-blown bottles every day – and dumped huge quantities of waste glass directly into the North Sea. Now, a century after the factory quenched its furnaces, that glass is being returned to us as something wanted.

Sand gathered, heated, made crystal and strong, then disposed of again and embraced by the tides. A relay team between industry and ocean: too much treasure to fill any sweetie jar, and the promise of rare shades not found on the average town-side beach.

'Milk-glass' is one of the special types of glass that can be found at Seaham. It is sought-after because of its opacity – but to me, this seems like surely it would defeat the main allure. With it, you cannot hold the sun between your finger and thumb.

Another rarity at Seaham is safety glass. That old-style of reinforced window – the kind you see in the door of a community centre: wire mesh suspended inside a sheet of liquid glass. Fragments of this remind me where the tempting gems have actually come from. But I like the transformation – the clean black line slicing through a drop of muted light.

Andrew and I edge our way north – moving slowly away from the town – where the glass pickings are sparser and less frantic. We move closer to the waning tide and find a few larger pieces. We laugh when, in our concentration, we forget about the chase of the occasional wave and dash suddenly from its foaming fingers. I think of all the jagged edges in my jar, softened only at the corners, tossed, likely, for just a few short years in the rip.

Here, some pieces are like marbles. Smooth and round, translucent after the recent lick of the sea. They remind me of the pearly beads Mum used to have – dollops of glass that went in water, in a vase of flowers, or a dish of floating tea-lights on the dining table.

Soon, we start to think about lunch. We turn our course back towards Seaham, the wind now behind us, pushing us towards the town. But progress is slow. I can't shake the feeling that I'll miss a perfect piece of sea glass if I lift my eyes too long from the ground. My raincoat pocket is heavy and jingles when I shake it for Andrew to demonstrate my bounty. He came along happily but without much interest in my beach-combing plans. Now the searching has gained an edge of competition.

The sea is grey and rumbling, and the wind has swept away the headache that had been lingering behind my eyes since this morning. I crunch through the shingle, forcing myself to straighten my neck every once in a while, to absorb the horizon. Living relatively land locked now on our small island, I try never to take a visit to the coast for granted. No matter the beach, it always feels like meeting an old friend. It would be rude not to pay it some attention now.

Groynes interrupt the shore, their blackened stumps limping into the water. The terrain turns sandy, and eventually I relinquish the hunt and we climb the dissolving concrete steps back up to the promenade. The sky has pooled its resources; the cloud gathering grey into deep, laden blue.

After a brief sweep around the main street and a quick look at the old harbour, we climb gratefully through the doorway of a fish and chip shop and manage to grab the last table at the back of the restaurant. We treat ourselves to hot, sugary tea, thick-battered haddock and copious piles of yellow chips. I order some sliced white bread and butter, and a can of orange Fanta. A large family with two highchairs and a mound of different coloured raincoats talk over one another. An older couple across from us coach their two grandsons through the ritual of this timeless fish-supper feast.

I sit back, smiling and stuffed, against the red-leather booth seat. I think about how much a part of the landscape our presence is. Places are not separate from people – not on an island like ours. Places are a collection of stories. They hold each chapter in their hedgerows, their forest floors, their bricked-up river banks and their cake-layer cliffs. They hide it in their shingle; not hard to find when you take a moment, a proper look.

When we were living in Manchester, during the pandemic, scouring the Castlefield canals for optimism, I was also trying to complete my master's in creative writing. Classes had been swept online, and I was reading a lot – books that spirited me to evergreen forests, gale-blown beaches and frosty meadows.

It was around this time that I began to consciously write non-fiction. I had in mind a piece that gathered all my favourite swimming memories, and that would, while I wrote it, transport me to the places back home, in Wales, that I couldn't physically reach. But once I entered the deepest waters of the essay, I found that it was actually about something else. I gave it the title 'Return to Water', and it became a cathartic dive into my own unexamined journey towards womanhood. It was a piece that brought the outside world onto the same pages as my private self.

The work was surprising, difficult, and it began a chain reaction of ideas that would, one by one and over a handful of years, become their own essays.

Often, my intentions would shift like sand dunes as I typed – mapping new thoughts onto old landscapes: lakes, leisure centres and childhood kitchens. I was collecting sea glass; looking for glints of coloured meaning, watching them change with the light, arranging and then rearranging them until they made a shape that seemed to matter.

And somewhere, pretty far along the line, I noticed that I have always been collecting: shells, fossils, photographs and half-finished notebooks. I am a library of things. I am made of places and of other people: songs, Sunday afternoons and long conversations; everything pressed, like wildflowers, into the pages of a book.

The drive home from Seaham to York is warm and heavy-muscled. Back in the kitchen, I take a pale blue dinner plate from the cupboard and carefully empty out my pockets. Glass clatters onto ceramic glaze.

Lots of the colours, I notice, have transformed as they have dried. The depth and lustre of the glass I found on the beach has evaporated with the sea and rainwater. Lots are frosted as if with fine sugar – like pear drops. One, more like granulated sugar – a lime fruit pastel.

Among the ocean blues and greens, there are wire-crossed pieces, like fragments of crystallised graph-paper. And some surprisingly satisfying nubs of milk-glass, collected for their bright hospital-scrub colours and pleasing weight. I even have a two-toned treasure: pale soaking into dark, the colours of an iceberg disappearing into arctic depths.

The largest piece, almost like a marble in its roundness, is an unusual shade. It's the colour of the jelly between pork and pastry. A pale, oaty-rose colour, sugared but still translucent.

I separate off the orange colours: these are mostly nibs of flint, that, under the slick of rain and tide, were bright as amber, and so, breaking with tradition, they made the cut. I notice that a few redder pieces, gathered for the belt of black in their smooth surface, have dulled to the colour of clay brick, their stripes now grey like grout. I find it hard to believe that these polished kidney beans were once a red-brick building, but it's possible.

I sit back and survey my collection. I think about how quickly it all wears down, from bottles and rubble into pretty jewels. Since Seaham stopped supplying its waves with glass a hundred years ago, the beach's bounty has diminished. Locals talk about childhoods kicking through a rainbow of glowing shingle, but now each year it takes longer to fill a fist with treasure.

I realise that when it's all gone, it won't just be because of the popularity of the place; it will be because the marbles have worn to beads, and the beads, at last, to grains of sand.

The waves roll on. Seaham sea glass will be distributed to windowsills and jewellery boxes all over the world. And the rest will be tumbled down to dust – just as it was before.

ST GOVAN'S HEAD, BOSHERSTON.

5.10 P.M.

The light is buttery, and the air is thick and still. The jackdaws are quiet, along with the slow-rippling sea below. You can hear a bee, heavy and tired, browsing the dry heather bells. Further off, inland, a car door shuts, and then another. Every minute or so, there's the drum of a nearby wingbeat as the gulls come in to their familiar crags.

The vast pool of milky sky soaks into the jade horizon. You stand motionless, trying to find some movement in the air, some perceptible bristling of the hair on your arms. But nothing. All is calm.

The stacks, the rocks and the mulling sea, are waiting for the thunder to arrive.

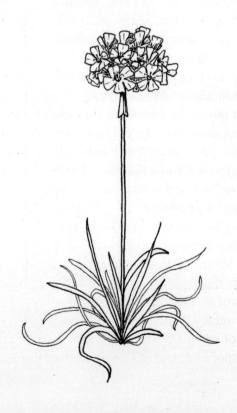

RETURN TO WATER

I

It's just gone 8 a.m. Padding carefully across the wet tiles, I breathe a sigh of relief. Only three other swimmers are here today. I slip into the water with an intake of breath. My new local pool is a little on the chilly side.

I fiddle with my goggles, press them uncomfortably into my head, and, as always, I begin by submerging myself completely. I observe my foggy surroundings, notice the sensation of water shifting in curls around my skin, and relax into the isolated quiet. Then I swim; languorous breaststrokes, letting myself drift deep below the surface between each rise for air. I like this bit – it's the closest thing I have to a ritual. For the first few lengths of every visit, I immerse myself. By the gentle press of water on my flesh, the slow buoyancy and support, I am reminded of why I am here.

The sky is bright this morning, and as I swan through the

centre of the pool, beams of light quiver in the cloudy blue in all directions. Another swimmer arrives. I break into front crawl, find my rhythm, and let my thoughts roll on with the soft momentum of my strokes. One, two, three, breathe. One, two, three, breathe.

We rely on water. Our settlements spring up around it. It is survival and renewal, power and transportation. It's cleansing, therapy, baptism and birth. It's 60 per cent of our bodies and 70 per cent of our planet. As humans, our relationship with water is a simple one. It's natural – a matter of dependence. Some of us are more dependent on it than others, I think, but all of us need water.

For me, being suspended in a lake, dipping my toes into the sea, watching the gush of a river or swimming lengths in the local pool – these things bring me back to myself in a way that's becoming rare in this loud and busy world. But my relationship with water has not always been a simple one. It is tightly knotted to my relationship with myself; my identity and self-esteem. For me, returning to water is like returning home; and yet, for almost a decade, crossing its threshold became difficult – sometimes even impossible.

II

In my family, I'm the runt of the litter, the youngest of four; and they all insist that I was a water baby. My mum remembers early bath times: I would get very excited, frantically waving arms and legs, happily splashing water out of the plastic baby bath. I can recall some of this excitement a few years later in the big tub. I would refuse to get out; instead relentlessly sliding up and down the ceramic on my bum, until all the water had drained away and I could slide no more.

Both my parents clearly remember the arguments over who was to take us to the local pool. Neither of them looked forward to the weekly Sunday outings. 'It was stressful,' Mum said, 'keeping an eye on you all. Your brother almost drowned on multiple occasions, and I'm sure there were rules about how many children you could supervise alone. We were always breaking that.'

What I remember are the orange armbands, filled with breath and pinching skin as they went on; the nappy smell in the changing rooms; the colossal slide that shot us out into the pool at what felt like a million miles an hour.

Slipping through the water now, it's strange to think that this movement needed learning. It's come to be so natural: my body adjusts to the gravitational change like a bird taking thoughtlessly to air.

My dad was often there in my most memorable swimming moments. He was the person I followed into most adventures. I remember when he lowered me down into a container tank at work and let me doggy paddle in the dark. Dad's workplace – a chemical manufacturer in Barry Docks – at that time had just had a new storage tank delivered to the warehouse. It was a huge, black metal block of a thing, as big as a house to my young eyes. Regulations meant that the tank had to be leak tested, which involved filling it up with water and letting it sit for fourteen days. He saw this as an opportunity: why waste all that clean water? So he asked if any of us wanted to go for a swim.

I, thinking it sounded like a brilliant idea, was the only volunteer. I remember my mum and my sister standing on the top of the tank with Dad as he lowered me down through the small opening and into the blackness. It was gaspingly cold. I giggled away, treading water in my armbands, a little scared of the void around me but never willing to admit it.

Sometimes, when I visit Dad's work, I walk past that

tank, sitting there now under a layer of dust, holding huge quantities of aluminium chlorohydrate. I'm taken, fleetingly, back to that bizarre evening, and it feels as though I could have dreamt the whole thing up.

By the time I was nine, I had decided that natural water was a thoroughly magical place to be. We went on a trip that year, to Canada, and for me, the fortnight spent travelling the Rockies was really just a swimming tour. The memory I always return to comes from one of the last days of that trip: we had parked up by a lake for lunch, and I had managed to wangle permission to go off and find the jetty by myself. Once there, I left my sandals by a polished log and ran. My feet barely skimmed the wooden planks and when I reached the end, I didn't stop, I didn't hesitate; I just jumped. I could feel hundreds of tiny bubbles fizzing about me, rolling up my skin and tickling my cheeks.

I opened my eyes in the fresh, green water and found myself surrounded by flashing fish. I had jumped straight into a shoal of them, and as they flitted about, I felt one brush my ankle, my arm, escape my hair. I stayed suspended for a moment, and then reluctantly resurfaced.

This is a memory I have painstakingly preserved, because to me, it was a perfect moment. Most thrilling was the fact that it belonged entirely to me and no one else. It was the first in a collection of moments in which I have been completely and blissfully present, in my body, cushioned from everything but myself, my happiness, and my glorious surroundings.

Any water would do, of course. Though we lived by the sea (the silty Severn Estuary, often out of reach beyond half a mile of mud) good natural swimming holes weren't too common. When I was seven, however, we moved to a house that could more easily fit all of us under its roof. And quite bizarrely, at the bottom of its garden, this house had a swimming pool. A survival of the fifties or sixties, lino-lined and rectangular, and very much still usable. On finding this out, the idea of having to leave my childhood home (the terraced house I had been born in) became much less of an injustice.

From then, I would spend my summer holidays in a constant state of either dripping wet or drying off. Friends would visit every day; I'd zoom lengths with my orange flippers; I'd dive for 'treasures' (a precious array of heavy plastic objects). We had an old, long, dressing-up box that my siblings and I turned on its end and used as a diving platform...a health-and-safety disaster, considering the pool was just over a metre deep. One year, we bought an inflatable slide for the poolside, but quickly discovered it was much more fun when used upside-down, in the water, as a giant floating seesaw we could all pile into together. The plastic was split before the summer's end.

I was eleven when I first looked at a photo snapped during one of these mad pool parties and felt unhappy about how I looked. This was before I had started wearing makeup; before I even really thought about my appearance from an outward perspective. But I clearly remember seeing my red face, goggled eyes, crooked teeth, and wet, rat-tailed hair. I remember the image re-surfacing in my mind when I next swam with my friends. It was then that I lost it: my sense of abandon slipped away. Water was becoming more complicated.

III

I concentrate for a while on my breathing, on the shape of my hands as they enter the water, the frequency of my kicks and the strand of hair that I can never prevent from plastering my face each time I turn to take in air. Swimming lengths is an easy way to be alone with your own mind. There's respite in the simple pattern of my movements, in the drag and ripple of my body as I swim. One, two, three, breathe. One, two, three, breathe.

I inherited the family tendency for acne at around the age of twelve. With it came a host of problems and anxieties, which across the years, were mixed-in with a cocktail of other adolescent battles, inextricable from one another and, ultimately, quite impactful on my way of life. I had a tricky and fragile relationship with my outward appearance, and it was the kind of unhealthy relationship that stopped me from being myself, from doing certain things, and from having certain conversations.

This is a story shared, I know, by many. Estimates of how many British adults have at some point suffered from acne (classified as one of the most common 'diseases' in the world) range to as high as 95 per cent. A survey published by the British Association of Dermatologists in 2018 strove to acknowledge the oft-minimised impact that acne can have. It reported that: '54 per cent of British adults who have ever experienced acne feel that it has had a negative impact on their self-confidence, and 22 per cent feel that it has had a negative impact on their social interactions.'

Most interestingly, the survey asked people a series of 'would you rather' questions, giving an insight into the real-world importance of the issue in people's minds. Twenty-eight per cent of those who had experienced severe acne said that they would rather see their chosen political party lose a general election than go through a month-long bout of it. Fifteen per cent would rather be in debt. Seven per cent would rather be dumped by their partners.

Aware that these findings would be surprising to some readers, Dr Nick Levell, President of the British Association of Dermatologists, insisted that: 'this shouldn't be viewed as a weakness, or anything of the sort, rather it is an indication of quite how awful an experience it is for many.'[1]

Once, in a heady summer of exam results and first loves, intoxicated with our own potential, I whispered to my closest friend that I would give my place at university away in return for 'normal' skin.

In every version of this story – whether its acne or any other difficult relationship with one's body – there's a private goalpost: the thing you always spend your wishes on. Swimming lengths in a standard chlorinated swimming pool, flanked by passing strangers, was mine.

When I was thirteen, I started wearing makeup every day; despite not knowing what to buy or how best to put it on. I had, by that point, fully acquired my 'problem skin', and the result was a growing sense of disconnection with my own appearance.

Makeup wasn't my mask. The version underneath – the red and sore and angry version that met the mirror before bed – was the false one. I couldn't be myself without the armour of my curated appearance, the careful ritual of my morning routine. Makeup gave me the freedom to face the world with confidence, and each year my skin grew worse it trapped me tighter into my dependence on those products.

And so it came to be that I couldn't submerge myself in water anymore. Of course I couldn't. It would jeopardise

---

1. This survey was released to mark the launch of The Acne Support website – a flagship acne resource providing information on acne types, causes, treatments, prevention, scarring, as well as emotional support, and practical tips for covering acne. Source: *www.bad.org. uk/over-half-of-people-who-have-ever-had-acne-feel-it-has-affected-their-self-confidence/.*

the careful control I thought I needed: it would wash away what held me up.

I was fourteen when I grew out of starring in the local pantomime, but I have a much-avoided memory of that final show that marks a point of no return. I had a follower that year: the six-year-old daughter of one of the adult chorus who had taken a shine to me. One evening, as I played with her in the village hall, I noticed her gaze become fixed on my mouth and jaw. Then she reached her hand up as I was talking, as if to touch my inflamed skin. Instinctively I caught her arm and gave it back to her, trying to continue as if nothing had happened.

But then, eyes still fixed, she said, 'What's that?'

'What's what?' I replied, pretending to be oblivious.

'What's that on your face?' she said.

I could have calmly explained to this little girl that acne is something that lots of teenagers experience…But she had done what I feared most when I was with other people: she had noticed. She had made me naked to attention, ruined the whole façade. I caught another outstretched hand and told her not to point.

'You shouldn't say that to people,' I said. 'It's rude.'

For the rest of the rehearsal, I let my hair fall onto my face, and tucked my chin into my scarf. I felt, as I would feel for many more years, a desperate need to hide my skin. Until that point, I had often told myself that other people might not see it, that my cheerful self and buoyant voice would camouflage my insecurities. The little girl had meant no harm, of course, she had only said what she was thinking. But this was the problem: it meant that other people thought the same, they just didn't say it.

As I grew older, I learned how best to hide. I was good at it. No one would have said I was shy. My mum understood how important makeup was to me. She helped me buy the right products, researched with me, supported me when I couldn't pay for the skin-sensitive ranges – and took me to the GP when I had appointments for my acne. Gradually, I honed my skills, and was able to make it all look 'natural' for school.

The years I spent hiding, I also spent pretending there was nothing to hide. Even my language was part of the effort. I couldn't bring myself to utter certain words or make any kind of reference to my skin. Spots, acne, pimples, zits: even typing them here, now, pushes up against my instincts.

Each word had the power to break the spell, to make me suddenly bare to other people's searching eyes. I never talked about it to my friends. I never took my makeup off. I never drew attention to this fact. I lived in complete outward denial of the thing that, secretly, ruled my life.

It was easier to forget how much I loved to swim. I stopped visiting the local pool – that was far too stressful. I could still go to the sea with friends, but I had to turn myself into the person who only waded in so far, while others splashed and messed about. The few times I was invited on a Friday night to the big new pool with curly slides and disco lights, I made my excuses. To be wet was to be anxious – it reminded me of the fragility of my performance. I didn't belong to my own bare skin. Swimming no longer gave me power, it threatened it.

IV

Staying dry didn't sever me from water altogether. Living just minutes from the sea, having it near, was important to me. In my stressful years at sixth form, with older siblings all flown, I would go west with my parents at weekends. Access to the open horizon and to the smell of salt is a time-tested antidote for almost any inner strife.

I seldom worried so much about my appearance in these places. Our little corner of Pembrokeshire was a forty-eight-hour escape from fashion and from my reflection – time spent in fleeces, wellies, and away from the floor-to-ceiling mirrors in my teenage bedroom.

Nevertheless, even during those times, I don't remember spending more than twenty-four hours without any trace of makeup on my face. For my Gold Duke of Edinburgh expedition, we were told to take *only the essentials*. I was small for my age, meaning my maximum bag weight was small too. But I had to make room – I couldn't go four days among classmates without it. I couldn't go four minutes.

I felt shameful about how important it was to me. Spending the night over at other people's houses, perhaps after parties (or even, later, with my first boyfriend) meant sneaking to the bathroom early, before anyone else woke. To apply just enough makeup to feel comfortable, but not enough that – heaven forbid – they notice and think me vain or pathetic.

The general attitude is that makeup is a trivial thing; *certainly not worthy of an essay's worth of words*, as I've told myself many times while writing this. And yes, absolutely, I hope that for lots of people it is trivial. But for some of us, it's the symptom of a bigger issue. We have normalised the act of changing our appearance in order to feel comfortable or accepted. In fact, we've encouraged it.

You can now quite easily transform the way you look – affordably and with remarkable results. This, I believe, is an amazing choice to have. Makeup is art and it is liberation. In the queer community, for instance, makeup is nothing short of powerful. It's part of a vital movement in having control over how we present ourselves. I would describe my own use of makeup as liberating too: in so many ways it freed me and allowed me to go out in the world with confidence. This sounds like a paradox – and that's because it is. Every makeup wearer knows what that relationship with the world's gaze means to them, and for each of us it's slightly different.

I want us to acknowledge what might happen when that opportunity for control becomes the controller. In other words: what happens when someone becomes trapped by a *need* to look a specific way? I am part of a society, founded in misogyny, that has conditioned me to care deeply about my appearance. And yet, when in those depths, problems evolve, I am told that matters of appearance are trivial, surface-level, shallow.

I would be the last person to criticise the existence of makeup, but I wonder why we seldom seriously discuss the role it plays on both a societal and an individual level – especially among the younger population. We quietly shun young girls when we see them batting heavy fake lashes and puckering outlined lips, but we hardly ever consider why these rituals exist – and even less frequently do we consider what that individual girl's relationship with her natural appearance might be.

The reality is that for many people, control over their appearance really does matter: particularly those who are not yet at home with their bodies. In many high school culture clusters, outward performance and visual impression are extremely important, and have massive impacts on the young people entwined in those systems. The widespread dismissal of this importance is one of the main reasons I failed to properly address or overcome my own hurdles for so many years.

And here's another truth: the people who wear the most face paint, spend the most time on their hair, and take the most selfies, are not the confident, vain or self-loving ones; they're usually the opposite. They are the people desperate to escape how they think they really look, and desperate for a moment of external reassurance – however fleeting.

V

I stop swimming, feeling distracted and frustrated. My goggles have fogged, so I lift them off. I fiddle with the straps to hide the fact that I'm also there to catch my breath. I try to stop my chest from rising too high as it drags in air.

The pool is getting busier with people who don't have offices to go to: the elderly and retired, the shift-workers, the self-employed. I try to time my visits in the lull between the early morning horde and this late-morning crew – the quiet window when the tiles are being hosed, the showers cleaned, the chemical levels checked.

I'll stay a few more lengths, I think. I'm not done yet.

When I left my home in the Vale for Durham University, I missed the sea in a way that showed me how lucky I had been. I often walked the paths along each side of Durham's winding river. In that first autumn, I watched, in awe, the salmon leaping with defiance up the weirs, bent on going further yet inland.

Living in a college was hard. While others rolled out of bed and into the dining hall for breakfast, I set my alarm earlier, applied my basic warpaint, and then pretended I had done the same. Suddenly, I had very little respite. I was surrounded by friends most hours of every day. I had to work harder not to show the seams in my appearance.

Along with the south Wales coastline, I had also left behind my referral to dermatology at the hospital in Cardiff. Throughout those high school years, I had been secretly battling through GP appointments, prescription creams, and countless rounds of unhelpful antibiotics. It took until I was eighteen to get the referral I needed. My compulsion to disguise hadn't helped; I couldn't articulate my issues; I couldn't admit them to a doctor or explain how they made me feel. I couldn't even bring myself to go without my makeup to an appointment.

In that final year of sixth form, I had watched a close friend's acne disappear from his cheeks. When I finally asked him about it, he advised me to be honest. 'You have to spell it out for them to really listen,' he said. 'You have to say that it's affecting your mental health.' Back then, I wasn't even honest with myself. I thought he was telling me to exaggerate the situation.

Eventually, I had found the guts to take a picture with me. It was an awful photo. It looked nothing like *me*. I held my phone up to the doctor and told her all I wanted was to go to university free from all this anxiousness. The waiting list for dermatology was six months long, and, when finally they named a date, I was 300 miles up north. I was taken off the list and told to start again in County Durham.

I lost all motivation then. I gave up trying. I had always maintained a certainty that one day it would stop; that I would just grow out of it. I told myself a thousand times it wasn't that bad, that other people had it worse, that I was being self-obsessed or over dramatic. I had been telling myself for years that this was only temporary, and that if I could make it to my twenties everything would be alright. But soon I was nineteen, and there hadn't been a single day for seven years that didn't begin with new and painful spots. I was trapped behind the hurdle of my morning routine, and things weren't getting any easier.

One September afternoon, a week or so before my second year at Durham began, Dad and I went for a cycle to the sea. It was a sunny day in Pembrokeshire, and we were heading for our favourite bay; just along the coast from the stack rocks at St Govan's.

By the time we hit the grassy path leading down the hidden valley, we were hot and tired and unstoppable. This wedge of coast has water as clear as the Mediterranean – though somewhat colder. Our secret little beach – blasted into existence in World War II, and now tucked safely beyond a 'WARNING: EXPLOSIVES' military sign – is a swimmer's small paradise.

We left our clothes on the rocks, socks shoved into trainers, and met the Atlantic at a sprint. It soon slowed me into an eager wade, and when my thighs twitched in sharp reaction, I threw my shoulders in.

Dad swam further out to the mouth of the bay. I let myself drift and tread until my toes could no longer scrape the sand. I leaned back, felt my hair spread, the back of my head cradled by the cold. I let my feet float to the sunny surface, my ears go under, and all was quiet. I could hear the muffled whooshing of my circling hands. My eyes fixed on the sky. I stopped paddling with my feet and let my body be held by the saline water. The rocky walls of our secret bay climbed into my peripheries each time the swell fell away.

My hands started making swirls in the water again as I worked to keep my face above the surface. I thought of my friends earlier that summer, diving into the waves in Cornwall while I waded in and prayed that at least some of my 'waterproof' foundation would survive. They spent the whole week showing their faces to the sun, gathering salt and freckles on their skin. *Why would I wear makeup? I'm on holiday! I'm having a break from all that.* They didn't know how alien such a thought was to me. They didn't know how the words, thrown into the room like laughter, made me burn with envy.

I could see Dad diving under, resurfacing, shaking the droplets from his lashes and swimming without a care. I closed my eyes and pushed the sea above my face.

Surrounded by it, completely, for the first time in years, I swam without thinking. I let myself be present in that simple, water-induced way. I swam without my old, relentless, illogical fears, and I didn't collect them again until we came laughing back to the shallows.

On my return to university, I went to see a practice nurse in Durham. I rehearsed my speech and had my photos at the ready, but still I smiled and held the worst stuff back. 'I suppose it's not as bad as others have it,' I finally said, an echo of my previous GP.

Instead of nodding in agreement, Nurse Jane asked me my age. Then she looked me in the eye and said: 'Kathryn, no nineteen-year-old should be afraid to leave the house.'

I was about to correct her, explain that I wasn't afraid, I just needed makeup. And then I realised that, for the first time in all this, someone was seeing the heart of my problem, not just its symptoms. A lump swelled in my throat. Without any further questions, Jane recommended me for referral.

VI

I reach the point in my swim where I feel as though my lungs have learned to breathe underwater. I pace through my strokes with a mindless and unbreakable rhythm.

The ebb and flow of my attitude to getting help has been complicated. It's been tangled up with stubbornness, optimism, and conflicting information. What followed were almost eighteen more months of barriers; some external and some built entirely by me. At the hospital clinic I saw an excellent dermatologist. But the drugs he prescribed had me sitting in the nurse's office two days later with an angry rash climbing like ivy up my legs.

We were left with only one remaining option: a notorious medication that I had seen my sister struggle through. Any quick Google search will throw up stories of depression, anxiety, fainting, peeling skin, even suicide – all surrounding the clinical use of Isotretinoin. It was the same drug that my friend had found success with back in sixth form. My sister had been unlucky, but we were so alike, and I was afraid...I genuinely feared that I didn't have the emotional resilience to weather something like that – not while also navigating my life at university.

I had been told the worst of it and, most crucially, I had seen others struggle with the most common side effect: red-raw skin unable to bear the touch of products. It seemed that taking the course would be at least six months without my warpaint. Unthinkable.

What I wanted, more than anything, was to be the kind of person who could wake up in the morning and make a choice. I wanted to be able to get out of bed and go outside; to cycle to the sea and dive straight in; to spend a holiday in the sun without the sting of product in my eyes. Nevertheless – thinking that perhaps I just needed a change of mindset – I tried to ride it out once more. Any day now, I thought, things would start to improve – and in the meantime I just had to learn to care a little less. This, of course, was easier said than done.

By twenty-one I'd had enough. I went back to the dermatology department and was seen by a doctor who barely looked away from her computer screen. She told me I couldn't have the final drugs, that I needed to rule out all the other options first. I told her I had done it all, tetracycline, oxytetracycline, doxycycline and lymecycline, that I had tried for years and couldn't do it anymore. She sent me back to my GP surgery with a letter telling them to try again.[2] I cried to my sister on the phone, and then to my mum, and then decided this was not the end.

I knew by then that I was deserving of these people's time; I was entitled to whatever it would take to fix my problem. With the help of my GP, I battled on, and sped through one brief (and useless) antibiotic course before returning to the hospital.

To my relief, it was the clinic nurse who took me on from there. I saw her every month whilst undergoing treatment: as a young woman, I had to prove each time that I wasn't pregnant before I was allowed to access the next thirty days of dosage. Isotretinoin is extremely harmful to unborn children. To take the course I was required to take the contraceptive pill, and to sign an agreement saying I would abort any accidental pregnancy, should it occur.

But after each awkwardly supervised urine test, we would sit down together, and when she asked me how I was, I answered with the truth. With each small victory she shared in my excitement, and in the end, I was lucky after all: those last six months of treatment were, in some ways, the easiest of all. I wished that I'd been braver, sooner.

Isotretinoin drags the moisture out of your body. It leaves your skin extremely dry, your lips peeling, and every surface highly sensitive. This is the main reason most can't wear makeup, or any kind of product while on it – and some doctors even recommend not moisturising for the

---

2. In a study released at the British Association of Dermatologists' Annual Conference in 2016: 'Guidance [...] recommends that, unless an improvement in the patient's acne is seen, GPs should only continue to prescribe antibiotics for up to three months (90 days) before considering referral to a dermatologist.'

sake of speeding up the process, though I can imagine this would be akin to burning your wrist on the hob and then running it under a scalding-hot tap. The miracle for me was La Roche-Posay – a skin company that has developed a range of products specifically for those undergoing intense dermatological treatment. The range included an 'ultra-tolerant' foundation that I could safely wear throughout those months. This, along with many, *many* sticks of Burt's Bees lip balm, was what got me through it.

The most valuable thing that the treatment gave me – as unpleasant as its side effects could be – was time. I had never in my teen or adult life had a 'good skin day'. My acne wasn't violent, but it was relentless, and so I had never had the chance to know my face without it. It was just a part of how I looked. But having clearer skin during the treatment enabled me to reconcile myself with my reflection in the bathroom mirror. The difference was less stark; washing my face became a nightly intrigue, as each time I took away the paint and still retained a little more of *me*. It didn't matter so much that some mild acne might return after the drugs had left my system. By then, I was able to see beyond a breakout, and know that there was more to me than those surface imperfections.

So while the drugs left me feeling raw, they did finally mark the beginning of what would be my eventual return to water, to freedom, and to myself.

VII

It was one morning in the middle of my finals that I made the leap. I opened the front door at quarter to seven and stepped out into a sun-sparkled morning haze. I wore large sunglasses for small comfort and had my makeup in my bag for afterwards. I was unaccustomed to such early starts but the streets were perfectly deserted. I made it to the chlorine-scented foyer and half expected to get stares from the receptionist. I felt incredibly exposed, with my bare face and scraped-back hair; but the receptionist only smiled and said good morning. My heart thumped as I tried to navigate the unfamiliar changing rooms – a labyrinth of doors and pillars – and I was sure I should have taken my shoes off somewhere further back.

But I did it: I lowered myself into the deserted family pool. I swam slowly and uncertainly, back arched and chin held up above the spreading ripples. Then, feeling braver still, I donned my dad's old goggles, held my breath and sank below the surface. The moment, suspended quietly in the cloudy blue of a public swimming pool, was surreal; the most tangible mark of my progression towards a freedom I had given up on so many times before.

The next challenge was to learn to swim again. I knew *how* to, of course, but I felt like a heavy, clumsy tangle of limbs in the water, and my lungs certainly couldn't keep up with continuous lengths. I decided that absolutely everyone was better at swimming than me.

I went a handful of times again to Durham leisure centre before I left. When I moved back home to south Wales, I was armed with a degree, healing acne scars, and a determination to push on.

I couldn't face the idea of muscular, nose-pegged and hair-capped swimmers fitting in sixty laps before work, so I timed my trips to Barry Leisure Centre to coincide with the pensioners. I pushed down my paranoia that others might be watching me swim, or counting my rests, or looking too long at my red, goggle-ringed face. Gradually, I started to remember how wonderful the water made me feel, and soon that little girl running carefree down the jetty started to resurface.

I persevered. I spent a year doing breaststroke. And then one day I did *more than two lengths* of front crawl. I did nine lengths. The week after, I did more, and the week after that, I found a rhythm I could maintain. I would come home and announce triumphantly to my parents exactly how many lengths of each stroke I had done. This was all made easier because I had a car to use – I could drive within its safe walls to the centre, dash inside, quickly change, and then pour all my attention into the water around me, rather than the strangers. Gradually, I started to feel comfortable.

Since then, I have begun to collect my water memories again; embroidering more moments into my personal map of Wales, and beyond. These regular indoor swims have been like small, energising sips of life, while the oceans, lakes and natural pools are great big gulps of liberation.

There is a place, somewhere on the coast between Stackpole and Bosherston, that my family calls The Jumping Place. The exact location is a tenderly kept secret of ours, though I'm sure we're not its only guardians – in fact I've recently seen the spot referred to in a wild swimming guide.

If you walk towards the edge of the stubby-turfed cliffs – to the right bit of edge – you'll find that the rough green rug beneath your feet slopes downwards, becomes crumbled with hard rock. You'll peer over the edge of a sudden crater, gasp at its hidden size and depth and at the luminous water slushing down below. Then you'll clamber down steeper, rockier grass alongside it. You'll look up from your careful feet and see the deep, sparkling blue of the ocean framed by a natural archway in the rock. You'll climb down – though not easily – under the archway, emerging on a safe, staggered platform looking out to sea. The sun will have warmed the rock ready for your towel, and the water will be lapping lazily about twenty feet further down, depending on the position of the tide.

This is The Jumping Place. There are three easy levels to launch your flailing limbs from, each one perfectly positioned to let you drop straight down into turquoise bliss. Once in the water, you can tread and swirl and float and laugh, and admire another archway – this time dark and jagged, beckoning the entrance to that enormous crater stamped out of the cliffs. Then you can climb out, dripping and elated, being careful to not let the swell of the sea knock your knees on sharp barnacles (shoes are a must). Return to the ledge and repeat the process as many times as desired.

This is what I did, returning after a long interval, without jumping. I went, joined by my parents and Andrew, and launched my body from the land until the late summer sun cast us into shadow.

In north Wales, I swam with my oldest friend, who remembered better than I did how the water made me happy. She took me to a mountain lake – Llyn Padarn – and we bathed at sunset, surrounded by the shaded contours of Eryri. Everything was still. The water was so clean and cold, and laughter spilled freely from our uncontained smiles.

On the Llŷn Peninsula, I swam in the sun-warmed sea at dusk. I watched calmly as across the lilac bay a storm began to gather in the hills. I swam surrounded by new friends, talking and singing, tongues of seaweed licking at our ankles.

Back in Pembrokeshire, I visited the Blue Lagoon – an old coastal quarry made famous by its tidal pool – photos of which I had drooled over for years. Falling through empty air is an unnatural thrill, made all the more addictive by a sudden plunge into natural water. You have to force your reluctant body to make the leap, but everything that follows is freedom in its purest form. The lagoon at Abereiddy is a dark, beckoning blue. It feels bottomless when you look down on it from the quarry wall. We spent an afternoon there, jumping tirelessly like children, over and over and over.

I went on holiday with Andrew – the first proper poolside

break I'd been on since I was eleven – and insisted we stay somewhere I could easily leap into the Mediterranean Sea. I spent the days in and out of the water. My skin felt more sun, I think, than it ever had before. With my hands I rubbed suncream into my cheeks, without a mirror. And there is a photo of me, looking straight at Andrew from behind the camera, sun in my eyes and freckles on my face, my hair dripping in tendrils from the salt water. There's not a hint of hesitation in my eyes. It's just me, standing on hot rocks over glowing sea, my face decorated only with the happiness of the moment.

VIII

By the time the pandemic arrived in the UK, I was studying again, this time in Manchester, and swimming two, sometimes three times a week. That had to stop, of course. But though the next few months of lockdowns and travel restrictions kept me out of the water, they also did something else quite remarkable: they gave me a window of time more useful, even, than those months of medication had in Durham.

Being unable to swim for so long was hard, especially as I had become quite reliant on it as a therapeutic exercise: the focus on breath, the isolation in the water, the complete exchange of air and energy.

But those months spent in isolation, in our tiny little flat, were months when I actually stopped using makeup altogether. As our new reality settled in, so, gradually, did I. Every evening I was hitting new records for the greatest number of days without makeup, and every morning I was waking up with more and more familiarity with my bare reflection. I was getting used to it; my eyes no longer looked small without eyeliner, my lashes no longer short without mascara, or my eyebrows sparse without pencil. Once upon a time, I had almost forgotten what I looked like without makeup. By May 2020, I had almost forgotten what I looked like *with* it. Finally, I had completed the process that Isotretinoin had simply started: I was reconciled with my natural appearance. And for the longest time since I was a child, my skin had been able to breathe. Not just on a beach or in a lake, but all day, every day.

Of course, the pandemic brought with it a whole spectrum of unwanted change – but despite the cost, my silver lining is a very real one. I know I wouldn't have had the conditions necessary to build such a comfortable relationship with my skin again had it not been for 2020.

Today, I woke, dressed, scooped up my swimming bag and walked straight out into the dark morning mist without a second thought. I arrived at the leisure centre with bare skin and greasy hair. I changed absentmindedly in the locker rooms, clipped back my fringe and walked, blinkered, past the floor-to-ceiling mirrors and into the chlorine haze of the pool area.

Of course the journey continues: it hasn't been long since this was all a carnival of anxiety for me. I still have days when I lose a bit of courage; when I search the faces of the other bathers for their judgement; when I swim badly, get frustrated, and then catch myself in the mirror post-shower looking lanky and cow licked.

Easing through the water now, I ache for my past self. I regret the years I lost to fear, how long it took to find my way back. I remember – though I've made a habit to forget – the desperation of the girl who wanted more than anything to be able to leave the house without her armour. I remind myself that *here I am*.

It's almost nine o'clock. As I gently float myself towards

the ladder, I return to one of my most enduring memories. I remember standing in the warm evening seawater on Tenby North Beach. The tide was coming in, and I was singing the chorus of a Blondie song to myself, over and over.

I don't know where my parents are in this scene, but I know that I was concentrating on the caress of the sea around my legs. I was looking all the while at the rusting ladder fixed to the harbour wall, singing grown-up words about rising tides and holding on; about not giving up. The overwhelming aspect of the memory is contentment. I must have been about six at the time.

And then I remember my brother, having just pillaged the Fudge and Rock Shop at closing time, wading over to me and offering a chewy red sweetie from a paper bag. It was shaped like a pair of lips and tasted like soap. The sun was low, and the clouds were the colour of an unwrapped Barratts Fruit Salad.

I take my goggles off, submerge myself once more, and relax my eyelids under the gentle press of the water. Satisfied and ready for the day, I climb out of the pool and, humming quietly to myself, tip toe back across the tiles to the changing rooms.

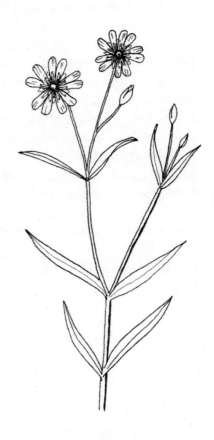

TŶ NEWYDD, CRICIETH.

5.15 A.M.

The sheep are wide awake. You sit on the edge of the cold stone wall in your pyjamas. There is a prickle of water in the air and the cloud overhead is tight and grey. Behind you, there is a breakthrough of blue sky, its corners gilded with some distant, peachy light. You picture the low sun igniting the tops of pillowy peaks, for someone, stretching stiff beside an aeroplane window, to lift the shutter, look down upon and admire.

Here, the light is muted and evenly laid over the ground. There is a chilly breeze.

The chitter of a magpie in the oak tree. Further off, the croaking of that same crow again.

The singsong seesaw of a chiffchaff, and the tinkling voice of a blackbird.

You see none of these creatures, but you hear them. You also hear the occasional pass of a car on the road below. You wonder where they would be going, so early on a Sunday, so close to the open sea. You hear the wind through the trees and somewhere, under all the morning noise, you think you can hear the rush of river over rocks.

There is a spray of late herb robert at your feet.

Yellow is diluting to an ordinary cream, the morning already losing its special quality; so soon. You stand, collect the folded towel you had placed between you and the wall's hydrated moss. You close the little door behind you and climb back under the duvet.

PEARLY QUEEN

There is a video, taken from a seat in the Paget Rooms in Penarth, of a five-year-old making her debut. The thick, felt curtains ruffle where they meet, and a little girl steps out. Her stout body sparkles with the waistcoat her mum has decorated for her: black velvet, bejewelled with a hundred stick-on sequins, bordering the seams and spelling 'Mum' and 'Dad' on each front pocket. Family members in the stalls know that on her back, inside a large sequin heart, are the initials 'KT'.

The little girl is alone, centre stage, hands in fists at her sides as she surveys the audience. You can feel the nervousness of the grown-ups behind the camera who think that surely, at any moment, some stage fright will kick in.

Her brow is furrowed, but her chin is raised. At last, the tonking piano arrives and the frown is replaced by earnest concentration. She releases the song she has been practising: each line is delivered loud and clear, surprisingly in tune, and almost always to time – though the pianist is kind and responsive. The lyrics also come with corresponding actions, like marching on the spot and waggling a discerning finger to the audience.

The little girl startles her supporters with a confidence that nobody has taught her, but which carries her through the first verse and onto the second, when the curtains open to reveal the rest of her dance class joining in behind her. Tap shoes tap on the painted wooden stage. A clatter of Pearly Kings and Queens in varying degrees of glitter.

Jane Clark's School of Dance meant Tuesday evenings above Albert Road Methodist Church. It was knitted pink ballet cardigans, wrapped across rounded tummies after teatime. It was small feet whizzing about in elasticated pumps – gone grey on dusty floorboards – and it was hand-me-down tap shoes scraping on the stone steps up to the hall. I attended Jane's classes from the age of about four until just before my nineteenth birthday, by which point she had become one of my oldest friends – and a great constant throughout the rippling years of my young life.

Each summer, we would put on a show. The huddle of dressing rooms hidden behind the Paget Rooms stage would be filled with squealing girls. Dances were performed by groups of every age, some songs returning every year, each cohort taking their turn to step 'On the Sunny Side of the Street'. Often there would be themes and costumes: a plastic shell-shaped paddling pool for the class doing 'Under the Sea', carried on by the older girls to reveal a tiny blushing mermaid; white caps for the cast doing 'Drunken Sailor', a motley crew of children wielding plastic brooms from Woolworths.

For two years running, our numbers spilled into the storage room beneath the stage, where we clambered up onto a mountain of dusty rolled-up carpets. Our laughter could be heard by families in the stalls throughout the evening – despite the brave chaperones' best efforts.

The shows were put on for us and for our parents. There was a 'biggest smile' competition for the baby groups, and though no child returned home without someone else's socks, many went skipping and triumphant.

Every year, there would be talk of grades. We heard stories of other girls, *the older girls*, who had done the exams. Sometimes we practised set 'amalgamations' to a crackly cassette, each song introduced by a prim English woman's voice. But nothing ever came of it: the 'examiners' remained mythical beings. I know others who were frustrated by this, and parents who expected certificates. But I was privately content with the situation: happy to entertain the idea of progression, but not exactly keen to punt for the necessary stamp.

When I was ten, I joined a stage academy on the other side of Cardiff. There were kids of all ages, all vying to be good enough for a life under lights, all turning around in confusion when my unfamiliar name was called out for the part of Oliver Twist. I'm amazed by the bravery I must have had back then; I launched myself into the challenge, though it was fraught with pressure to learn lines, to take directions, to impress.

There were two other children sharing the lead role, both of whom were older and had done this sort of show before. Mum drove me almost an hour every Saturday to rehearsals. I was way out of the shallow warmth of Albert Road waters, but I was determined to succeed. The experience culminated in a performance at the Riverside Theatre in Newport. I had to leave school early, a small star among my class: the glamour of a show beyond the Paget Rooms, beyond the M4.

I remember an itchy wig, lights that extinguished the whole audience, and special sticky tape that pulled all the baby hairs from behind my ears and made my eyes stream when the show was over and it was time to take it off. If I had seen beyond the dazzle and blur of the whole experience, I would have spotted my sisters holding a make-shift sign: 'Go Katy!' in red lipstick letters, hanging over the upper circle balcony.

I stayed for another term or two, settling into the chorus and making a few friends, but after a year, I'd had enough. Forms were being circulated to pay a hundred pounds to have your name and photo in a casting catalogue. The word 'amateur' arrived in my vocabulary.

I liked the idea of stardom, but I hated the thought of failure. I had reached an age where I was aware of its lurking possibility.

Throughout my teenage years, I took increasingly larger steps back from the stage. My high school had a cavernous auditorium that was burgundy and beige and was famed across the county for its extravagant annual shows. But faced with the competition of popular peers, the gruelling after-school schedule of rehearsals, the colossal risk of not quite being good enough...in the end I found my happy medium in the wings. As a member of 'stage crew', I was where I loved to be: part of the musical, familiar with all the scenes and songs, but with none of the pressure to get it all right. I could join the fun a week before doors opened and celebrate the success on closing night.

When I had first arrived at the big secondary compre-hensive, where all my siblings had gone before me, I was blissfully unaware of how choppy its waters would be. In spring, I entered the school eisteddfod,[3] as I always had before, with a song. Making the final three, I was to perform it on the day for an auditorium, jostling with all twenty classes of my new year group. For three years, I persisted with this – despite not being one of the musical theatre 'girls', despite never winning the prize, and despite the taunts from certain boys in the dining hall – before I finally had the sensibility to give it up and retreat to safer shallows.

One of my good friends often baulks now at why, that first year, three of us had also entered the dance category of the St David's Day competitions. Hours of after-school meetings, discussion over music choice and outfit design, culminating in a meticulously choreographed modern-dance-tap-dance mashup.

'Why on earth did we do it?' my friend groans through her adult-tinted glasses. 'It was sooo embarrassing.'

I know exactly why we did it. Because, not knowing any better, we were having fun.

---

3. An eisteddfod, modelled after the National Eisteddfod of Wales, is a coming together of music and culture, with competitions in poetry and song. Most Welsh schools held them each year on St David's Day, and in primary school it was a major highlight in our calendar. I was older than I'd like to admit when I realised that it wasn't just the Welsh word for something everybody did – that there was no equivalent in English schools.

I'm stood in the middle of the grey linoleum flooring, where the last song ended. Jane is stood just apart from me, weight on one hip, arms crossed. We've been talking through a carousel of conversation topics, and the time slot which my five pound note paid for has long expired. The adult tap ladies are due to bustle in at any minute.

'Right,' says Jane, turning on her heel, breaking the easy cycle. 'Let's move onto your favourites, shall we?'

(Double pull backs, I think they're called, though we had a very relaxed approach to naming steps.)

I click my feet over to the left end of the lino floor and set my back to her. Right foot forward, knees slightly bent, weight hovering low over my back heel. I shift it forwards and then back into my heels again, testing the distribution, leaving just enough in my arches. And then I pull my body up and back two steps at once, letting the balls of my feet tap weightlessly, one after the other, clean and sharp on the fleeting ground, before landing again, fully planted. One movement, four distinct sounds. The whole thing is done in a flash, and even if you could slow it down, you would scarcely see the mechanics, or where those extra taps came from. I boggled at it for years: an enigma, a defiance of gravity that I would never understand.

I reposition my feet and then pull back again. I check the space behind me, then do five in quick succession. The fourth scrapes a little, but by the fifth, it's clean again. I land low with bent knees, palms faced out in front of me, as if pushing against a wall. I grin at Jane and laugh. It's only a few weeks since I cracked this secret code, and she's right: it's my absolute favourite.

At the end of my A Levels, I was taking weekly tap-dancing classes, alone with Jane, in the prefab community hall her little school had moved to. The grand old Methodist church had been bought by property developers for up-market apartments, with interior brick and archway features. What remained of the group I had danced with through the years had finally dissolved, but I had been unwilling to let go of the space that gave me movement and escape.

When at last I left my town and went to university, of course I took my tap shoes with me. Less than a week later, I would squirrel them away to the back of my bulging college wardrobe – and I haven't used them since.

Full of hope for finding some kind of tribe in tap, I signed up to the university Dance Society. I chose the intermediate taster session, reminding myself that though I don't have any qualifications, I *have* been tap-tap-tapping for about fifteen years.

When I arrived, the Students Union was filled with legging-clad (and even leotarded) students making probing small talk. Inside the studio, bags dropped into the corners of the room, and most feet donned creased lace-ups with loose-fitting metal plates.[4] The cluttered sound of 'warming up' soon rattled around the walls.

The session was frantic. Everything we were asked to do was a rush of noise, girls competing to click louder and faster than anyone else. I had seen this kind of tap before – a sort of stomping flamboyancy, perhaps taught in musical theatre. Names of steps were thrown into the room, met with knowing nods, while I searched other people's feet, to identify which amalgamation was expected. I learned the 'official' name for what Jane called 'I-like-sausages-for-my-breakfast' (a perfectly syllabled phrase to aid our rhythm)... and immediately forgot it again.

---

4. Though it's not really advised, not tightening the screws makes a louder 'clack' on the floor.

I left the room in mourning for what I thought I had lost. I never wanted it to be serious or competitive – or nerve-racking. I recognised, with a sadness, that my fifteen years were special for a reason I had only half-appreciated at the time. I archived it all safely away, and because it was easier, I decided to think no more about it.

A brand-new friend – in dungarees and woolly slippers – sings the lyrics to one of my favourite songs into a mic. She has a stickered guitar slung from her shoulder.

I'm stood at the back of a packed college bar, watching her perform. The notes, given to the room with such soft ease, begin to twang my own quiet vocal cords. I take another sip of my tinkling drink, and swallow down the sugary taste of jealousy.

Two terms later and I'm flirting with the thought of singing at one of these college *Unplugged* nights. We're in Miles's room, across the landing from mine. Grover is playing potential songs from his phone and Miles is fiddling with the capo on his strings. We share more music taste between us than anyone else in Block E, but I don't want to say yes to anything I can't fit neatly and comfortably into my vocal range. I'm trying to remind myself what my vocal range *is*; what it feels like. We start to experiment, and I sing a few words to myself, quietly, testing the sensation in my throat, the sound from inside my ears.

In my second year of university, I was pulled into the annual freppers-band: a group of musically inclined students yoked together to entertain the new freshers during their first week of social events. We had a few days to settle on some songs and rehearse them, during which a previous version of myself was coaxed out by the other members. The lead player was kind. The other singers laughed like we were family. When the drums and trumpet and guitars came in, it felt like anything was possible.

The point was to get everyone moving, singing, and to show the freshers that they had arrived in a place where anyone can have a go at this kind of thing. Singing with a band like that – *entertaining* people – was a total whirlwind. I found out that week exactly why performers do it.

By my third year, I was safely back in the wings of college productions, armed with a clipboard and a confidence in my ability to do my best work behind the scenes. My gig-playing career at Durham had been a short breath above the water's surface. I had ventured out under the lights in small and well-known spaces, with talented friends, and in front of a proudly welcoming community.

The bubble was safe and sweet. I savoured the moments as I collected them, knowing they would be only artefacts once out in the open sea.

There is a video recording from that year, made on a friend's phone: thirty seconds of me behind the mic. It makes me squirm, reaffirming all the times I chose to put my feet back on the ground and leave the singing to *proper* singers.

But there is also a photo: a quick snap of Miles, Grover and me, all in black-tie attire, laughing under college bar lights. I have one hand on the mic, the other in my trouser suit pocket, and a grin on my red painted lips. I smile every time I see this photo and can only assume that it was taken on the night we decided to share our slow-jazz, acoustic rendition of 'Crazy Train' by Ozzy Osbourne.

I sit opposite Emily after work, cradling the cool dregs of a mocha. I have been gathering the branches of my slow-grown anger and showing them to her. About how hard it is to see hobbies through to adulthood; about the cultural gap in organised fun once you are out of school or university; about how, in your twenties, it seems that any use of time needs to have one of the accepted justifications – robust rewards such as fitness, money, medals or friends.

'You know...' she jumps in '...you know, I found out recently that the word "amateur" actually comes from another meaning. It's something like, "for the love of it".'

She tells me that she started singing recently. I ask her if she performs, or anything like that.

'No, no, I just like it. But my dad has been in this weird band for years – he performs. I learned a song and I sang it to him and he said that at least I hit all the right notes,' she laughs. 'Thanks, Dad!'

The *Cambridge English Dictionary* defines 'amateur' first as 'taking part in an activity for pleasure, not as a job', and secondly as 'someone who does not have much skill in what they do'. I'd say that most of us think of the latter when we hear the word 'amateur', and that the term's connotations with enjoyment have somewhat fallen away in a world where everything is about outcomes.

Emily tells me that she has to leave by seven to catch a bus. She is going to try out a folk choir for the first time.

'They meet above a pub,' she says. 'I'm not sure what "folk" will mean exactly, but apparently it's good fun.'

Not long after that conversation with Emily, Andrew and I finally joined a gym in the area. This gym was what they call a 'health club', with courts and classes and regular activities organised. The young woman showing us around told me enthusiastically about the dance-related exercise classes they had. 'Everything we do is mixed ability, so you can start any time, any level.' I was there to see the swimming pool.

We walked the corridor past the tennis courts. I looked through the window into the cavernous blue light, trying to identify someone who might swing a racket like I do (something akin to swinging a frying pan) – someone with a bit less conviction.

'You can sign up to a fast-track tennis course when you join,' said the woman. 'They test out your ability in the first session. It's a great way to dive in.'

I raised my eyebrows at Andrew. When she went to fetch a pair of iPads for filling in the forms, he nudged me. 'You could do that,' he said.

'Mmm, no thanks. I'd rather just play with you.'

I had only recently taken up the racquet, and only with Andrew. He had always loved the sport, and I wanted him to have someone to play with during the pandemic. It was slow progress; quiet evenings on the community courts in our local park. With him, I was beginning to enjoy it – beginning to paint over all the terrible PE lessons, running after balls on the crumbling school courts: cold wind, cruel girls and compulsory shorts.

'Everyone else will be better than me anyway,' I said.

'You know, you don't have to be great at something to have fun with it.'

I get up from my desk and crawl into the low corner of the attic room. I try one of the boxes recently retrieved from Mum and Dad's. I try another, smaller one, and find a pair of small red ballet shoes covered in red glitter glue, worn when I played Dorothy in one of Jane's summer shows. Underneath, bedded among a trove of other childhood memories, is my Pearly Queen costume. The folded black bundle shows a flash of silver. I lift out the velvet waistcoat. Lots of the sparkles are gone. Understandably, Mum had bought a sticker cheat-sheet once she'd had enough of sewing sequins onto the skirt. But otherwise the outfit is just as I remember it.

I open the lid of a larger plastic crate, and there it is: a black drawstring bag with gold 'RV' letters printed on the front. I take my slippers off and lace on the tap shoes. They are stiff and a little too large – bought only a year or so before I stopped dancing, when using them each week still seemed an unquestionable fact of life. I pull the laces tight and get up onto my feet.

The immediate clack of hard metal on hollow wood is flinchingly loud in the small space. I test the heel plates, then the toe plates – four taps on the floorboards. Then, impatience flooding into my feet, I try the small, fast movements of a 'paradiddle'. One-two, three-four. One-two, three-four. I add more beats to the step, barely lifting my soles but speeding up the way we used to, clicking our feet with such ease, chatting while we warmed up our ankles. The sound is gappy and uneven. I stop.

I check the floor for dents or gouges in the grain. Soft wooden boards are not ideal for tapping, but the ceramic tiles downstairs would shriek horribly against the metal plates. I try another paradiddle, slowly this time, careful to meet each beat. I realise that after seven years, there are only scraps of muscle memory – skeleton patterns of familiar steps.

I stop again. The loud noise in this small space means I'm not using all my weight, hardly landing my heels. I decide, just for a moment, to make a racket for the neighbours. I stand in the middle of the attic room, where the ceiling is at its highest. One set. Not sausages, just beans. *I-like-beans-for-my-breakfast-I-like-beans-for-my-breakfast-I-like-beans-for-my-breakfast-and-I-like-them-for-my-tea.*

Not all, but almost every tap is there, each matching the rhythm of the words on my breath. An old, archived feeling arrives. I grin. I go again.

LYNDHURST, ONTARIO.

6.20 P.M.

You're just one extended foot from the water's flow, settled comfortably beside the creek. A pale, wood-clad cottage is perched quietly on the slope behind you. The evening sun is like a long-drawn bath, low and warm, and the shallow river slides ever so slowly around the bend. Water boatmen skim across its surface, twinkling the mirrored gleam.

You have a few tiny frogs for company among the puddled rocks. A quiet heron comes and goes from the boulders piled upstream. Purple mayflies. Blue dragonflies. The same black-cloaked turkey vulture sits politely in one of the taller trees, silent and alert.

You realise that there is no perceptible human sound. No lawnmower, no jets overhead, no cars in the distance. The tranquillity is hypnotic. You stay here for a while, letting go of time completely.

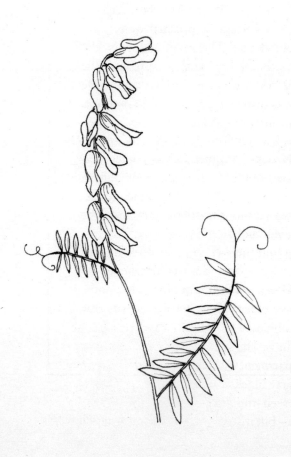

UNMOORED

Late September, 2018. I make my way along the edge of the wood and down towards the estuary. Glass beads shake from blades each time I tread. Skirting around some heavy nettles, I breathe greedily. I can smell the sun's gentle work as it lifts the dawn away.

I left the house at 8.09 a.m. Triumphantly early, but not as early as I had planned. It is fresh and calm, and I have overcome my fear of feeling silly or whimsical. It's rare to go out and break the dew without somewhere to reach, or a dog to exercise; with just the simple knowledge that this does me good.

My favourite thing about Porthkerry Park is the way that just as its trees give way to meadow, grass then turns immediately to pebbles. The rubbled bay itself is long and steep, reaching out at The Knap – or *Cold Knap* – where a huddle of pale apartment buildings sit. Today, they simmer in the distance: hazy blocks on the horizon.

I still haven't seen the sea – besides the silver flashes through the trees – but it strikes me as strange that I haven't heard it either. The pebbles are shored up particularly high this year, like the rim of a deep bowl.

Finally, I climb the dusty bank, thinking the tide must be low, and I stop. The steep-sided bay is filled to the brim. Three large logs float in the gold, like alligators in a hot lagoon. It's the highest I have ever seen the tide here.

And I can hear it now: the hushed lap of lazy waves on unaccustomed rock. I've met it just in time, before it turns away to start its next retreat.

I stop for a while and sit very still, balanced on the ridge, afraid of causing a clatter below. I close my eyes, sore with squinting, and listen.

My phone lies charging on my unmade bed. Aching to record the scene in some small way, I write a description in my mind, sift through all the useful words. But, just as a smartphone lens can't truly catch the colours of the sky, neither can our little language store the sounds of the sea. I settle on composing a message in my mind; something which sparkles with the joy of the jaunt, to be typed into WhatsApp when I get back to the house.

I think of it as a shame: that this moment of peace is witnessed only by me, that I can't share it with anyone, no validating its quality with exchanged words and mutual amazement.

I stand to go, being nagged away by the general assurance that there's something better to be doing than just sitting. Nine steps to the grass and it's gone, the sounds of the water tucked once more behind the wall of shingle.

January 2019. I shake off my battered umbrella in the entrance hall of Manchester Art Gallery. With my bag heavy on my shoulder, I carefully climb the stairs. I enter the first main space and begin to shyly stop at each painting on the wall. I'm unused to doing this alone. I'm afraid of looking out of place, or over-pensive, or worse, that I'll be bored.

But soon I find my pace, and, to my pleasant surprise, it's a slow and deliberate one. I linger over plaques; search the folds of each landscape and strokes of each face. For the first time, I stop at every single frame in each room – because I've got no one else to worry about. My usual experience of galleries and museums involves dipping my divided attention into a sample of what's on display. My mind is usually split by the tug of war between reflection and communication: processing information and socialising with my companions, each of us compromising around one another's interests.

I have the luxury today of too much time and terrible weather. I sink deeply into the collected works of the city, discovering enjoyment I didn't know before. My friends and relatives remain forgotten in my bag, and I accumulate new flavours of art, greedily, with my open mind.

When I emerge from the final collection, I head for the café, galvanised by the morning. I have decided to sit down for a hot lunch by myself – another endeavour I rarely, if ever, afford myself. I've been unplugged from my web of communication for a few hours now and I'm feeling comfortable. I've been anchored by the tactile stimulus around me.

But during lunch, my disconnection begins to feel more apparent. I can't hold the stiff pages of my book open with one hand while sipping soup with the other, nor can I focus on the words while conversations weave nearby. With rain dribbling down the window and steam unfurling from my bowl, my contentment spills over and I fish my phone out of my bag. Having resisted its company all morning, I can't keep the delight of the day to myself any longer.

I take a photo from my seat and send it to Andrew, who I'll be seeing in a few short hours. I glance around and then take another, considering the composition of an Instagram story. And with that, my lunch has gained an element of performance. I'm not cocooned inside the experience by myself anymore but split by my consideration of others looking on.

It's August, 2020, and I'm in my pocket of Pembrokeshire. I'm driving up the hill from Pembroke Dock, shopping bags on the back seat and all the windows down. The breeze is hot, and cars flood back from the beaches. I'm trying to decide whether my food will be too warm if I leave it in the car a while. I'm trying to decide if I can squeeze in another trip to the sea.

I know, at this hour, it will mean wading through the tide: struggling against the current of crowds leaving the coast and streaming down the narrow lanes in cars unused to reversing or passing quite so close. With no flights currently zipping off to Barcelona or Tenerife, there are more bodies on the local beaches than we have ever seen.

But high winds and thunderstorms are forecast for the next day, and my sticky skin is itching for the waves. To hell with the yogurt – I'll be quick.

The lowering sun floods my bug-splattered windscreen. I pull down the ceiling visor and lift my chin up to eclipse it. It seems that most of the holiday makers have already thrown in their towels, and I reach the thinned-out carpark without too much trouble. Door clunked shut, bag slung over my shoulder, I climb the stile leading away from the golden sands of Broad Haven.

My swim is swift and peaceful; I wade into the glimmering brine with less hesitation each day I come. I sink up to my chin, lift my feet off the sand, and wallow there in the craggy bay for a very happy ten minutes or so.

Afterwards I dry off and clamber back up the rocks. The small beach is shrinking with the evening tide, and a couple have arrived from the campsite with their spaniel. A man, lobstered from a day of sun and with a fishing rod mounted to his kayak, has also been coming and going, bringing crabbing nets in two by two.

I want to snatch some time to be alone with the rocks and the sea, and to absorb the colours properly before I head back to make dinner.

The water is dazzling: a mineral glow under the golden sun. The rocks are brushed with copper and the grass is glossy, glowing green. Everything is enhanced – even the wind is warm – like a high-saturation photograph. Pausing on the edge, I look back to the rocks I was just floating amongst. My phone is heavy in the pocket of my shorts.

I decide to capture this last hoorah of light, just once, knowing these kinds of colours are rare and precious for the average British summer. I know full well it will only store a flavour, but I don't want to forget how happy I feel, how uncomplicated, how spoilt.

This is what I fear when I pause to record a scene. I want to preserve it, because I don't trust my faulty human brain, crowded as it is with the constant building up and mulching down of memorable days. Even the sharpest moments, the ones which seem indelible at the time, are at risk of dissolving under the accumulating silt of it all.

Of course, I'd also like to have proof that I was here, that the beauty is real. I'd like to make people crave that flash of my location in return for all the times I've coveted theirs.

I take two pictures – one including more of the blue, the other more of the green – and then return the phone to my pocket and follow the rambling edge around further. There, the blue is deeper, with less shade muting the rocks. I snap three more pictures and keep my phone in my hand, frustrated by my inability to communicate to whoever might see these pictures quite *how* blue the ocean is. Just one well-chosen view will do the job – represent the evening without smothering it – but every hundred metres I find a new angle, a better view and light, and I choose that one instead.

I climb back into the car with a folder-full of photographs from the cliffs, but no lasting memory of how the air smelled, or which birds passed over my head.

I am spending August by myself. Much of the year leading up to it has been boxed into a small flat in central Manchester, while the world choked on its new disease. Our view was of the ring road and our soundtrack was the sports cars using its deserted lanes as a racecourse. We joked that the towering digital billboard across the way was our television, peering through binoculars in excitement when the pixels morphed into an advertisement we hadn't seen before.

All the minutes of all my days this year have been spent in the company of my teammate who, thankfully, I never tire of. But then Andrew's visa was due for renewal, and he was sent back to a homeland where visa centres are still very much closed. Not knowing how long he would be gone, we handed in our notice on the city hub that was draining our bank accounts and slotted our combined possessions into storage. Andrew flew out on an almost empty plane, and as people in the UK began to venture into one another's territories once more, I made my retreat to my own homeland; returning at last to my parents' cottage where I could keep up my freelance work – and finish my MA. I took myself into a willing isolation, craving and fearing the quiet of my own company in equal parts.

Spending a month in my favourite place, on my own watch and my own agenda, feels like the highest indulgence. My time is full of birdsong and swirling clouds and ripples in the sand – but rarely am I truly alone. Extracting oneself from society is hard now that it transcends space and time. Doing so is itchy and disconcerting. These days, my 'own devices' are disused and reluctant to engage. Being left alone with them is like being unmoored.

When I arrive back at the cottage, I'm hungry, but the last of the sun is creeping out of the tangled garden. I hover in the kitchen while my pasta boils, windows and doors wide open. The birdsong outside is raucous. Every tit and wren and robin is shrieking their song, calling out and joining the chorus. I stand at the window and wait, listening for a patch of quiet among the noise, but it doesn't come. The busy cacophony continues.

I drain my pasta and add the leftover ratatouille from the microwave. Outside there is a wooden picnic bench where I put my plate of food and my glass of squash. It is in front of the bird feeders and just in range of the Wi-Fi router.

On my way back inside, I pause, and consider for a moment whether to just sit and eat with myself, listening to the birds go to bed, thinking my own loose thoughts. But the idea of it feels uncomfortable to me – it has for years. I have a compulsion to be occupied, either with conversation or entertainment, while I eat. Over and over I give in, avoiding the daunting simplicity of spending a meal with just the taste of the food and my thoughts for company.

I fetch my laptop and place it on the wooden slat behind my plate. I angle the screen and turn the brightness up full.

I watch a young woman wake to the cold sunrise of an empty desert. I marvel at her bravery and independence, feel jealousy for her solo adventures that seem like the ultimate escape from all my tethers. And then I remind myself that I am there with her: I intrude via the rectangular frame that she has crafted around her day and shared with YouTube. Can you be truly present, completely in the moment, if your mind is crowded with an audience of strangers? I hope that this woman is able, when she wants, to zip up her camera bag and shut it all out. I hope she knows that her two eyes are more than enough, and that the pursuit of a flaming sky needs no justification.

The acts of recording and of sharing keep us stitched into a comfort blanket of technology and connection. They are brilliant powers to have, but they can also hold us a beat apart from the smell of damp clovers, or the strobed snatch of a bat at dusk.

I keep watching as the light fades around me and bugs begin to spiral through the open door, punting for the hallway light. I watch the screen long enough for my plate of food to empty, and for the recommended show to transport me quite unpleasantly back to times of high school romance. And then I close my laptop and go inside.

Outside the evening continues its chaotic opera, the birds performing their bedtime finale for all the closing buttercups, the weary cows, the first dinting stars.

I start the next morning by checking my phone, send a message to Andrew, and then slip into an unexciting scroll through Instagram. Outside the mist is jaundiced by the hidden sun. Eventually, I run out of things to check, and I push myself to follow through with the plan. I go for a run.

Running is not something that comes naturally or cheerfully to me. For the brief periods I have flirted with it, distraction has been important to success. This morning, however, I leave my headphones on the kitchen table. I have quelled the 'safety' argument with the knowledge that I wouldn't have any signal around here anyway, that I'm not venturing far, that for millennia, people have safely left their homes without the floatation device of a mobile phone.

I jog down the grassy driveway and turn left up the old lane. The morning is still gloomy here beneath the trees, and rotten bits of branch and twig snap beneath my trainers. I feel a chill in my shoulders. The slope increases. I wind up between the sunken banks of this ancient road. I strain to listen to the sounds beyond my heavy breaths and thumping feet. These twists and turns always have me on edge, each one an empty threat of unexpected walkers or sudden car engines.

I am here. I am heaving my empty stomach up the hill.

My jog is brief, cut short by lethargy and impatience, but I'm pleased that I have endured it alone. When I turn to head back, I pause, breathe in the smell of the fields behind the hedges, and notice the haze thinning out above me. I enjoy the downward battle more and manage at least some meandering thought amid the fixation on my aching legs. Back home I shower slowly, planning my outfit and meals for the day, then fry an egg and fold it in a slice of toast.

And then I go outside with my cup of coffee, and I stop for a moment. The mist has cleared and the birds flit from the feeder, to the tree, to the bush, to the feeder. I sit down. I close my eyes, let the sun dry my hair, and I listen.

Being unmoored can be itchy. It can feel like being adrift, cut loose from the easy and the familiar.

Slowly, year by year, I have become increasingly aware of a shift in the wiring of my brain. I see it in the people around me, too, and have talked about it at length with friends who feel the same. We all know it's there. We all marvel at how quickly a human mind can dig the groove of habit.

Things are so easy to avoid now. We don't have to be bored, lost, forgotten or uncertain. Our questions can be answered when we need them to be: How do I make pastry? What is the name of the flowers growing from the cracks in the garden wall? *Where are you? Are you okay?*

And I can preserve my life in high definition; precious pressings of time and the people I love, of who we are now but will never be again. I can quell the nagging feeling that I'm wasting something good, by making it eternal. Job done.

Being unmoored means dwelling in empty space.

There's no such thing as empty space when I have a steady supply of low-demand stimuli. Even the time it takes for a friend to finish '*typing…*' needn't be barren. But how important those little pockets of open thought can be. And how many interesting uses of that larger space we might have found.

I feel uneasy; as if there are important muscles I'm neglecting and letting waste. Escape is essential – any reader of books will tell you this – but so much avoidance, I am sure, is doing no good for my resilience. Understanding the various tangles of your interior takes practice.

I have so much power under the press of my thumb: an ability to archive endlessly and with inhuman clarity; to know every phone number and email address; to replace the unique filter of my imperfect vision and memory.

To distract from the noise of my emotions with the balm of endless content.

To distract from gaping silence with the noise of endless content.

To never be alone.

Being unmoored means dwelling in a singular experience. It means being what we are for a moment: individual.

Early spring, 2022. I climb the stile that separates the park from the fields beyond. It's the first time the air is carrying spring with it. The sun has some warmth to give, and I feel my armpits prickle under my jumper as I walk on. The river has returned to its usual level, leaving trunks, leaves and branches dusted with grey mud, and debris clinging to dead brambles. To my right there is a new pond in the field, swamping the grass and claimed by some opportunist geese. I follow the bank of the river Ouse, and I wonder how long it will take before the shrinking pond disappears again, summoned into the sky by the warming sun or absorbed by the filtering earth.

I have spent a day at my desk with my phone beside me, periodically igniting the screen in nothing more than an automatic habit. Without even unlocking the thing, I am surfacing from any kind of deep focus I might have been sinking into.

Concentration has become less comfortable in the years since leaving university. It means shutting out the multitudes. And there's my phone: beating black and empty in the corner of my vision, keeping me in the shallows with its tempting buoyancy.

I came out to remind myself, once more, that this is not wasted time. If I walk by myself I'll notice more, feel more, think more. As mammals, the way we can connect with one another is one of our greatest skills. But untethering myself and letting my thoughts form their own shape is vital, too.

The dictionary equates 'unmoored' with 'drifting', 'loose', or 'unanchored'. Drifting is what we do when we are passive: afraid of the depths, or reluctant to choose a direction. And yes, to be unmoored and without a paddle is a terrible thing: before long we could be lost, without any control or grasp. But I think that I would like to re-learn how to steer myself, to navigate the deeper waters. I would like to meet the wind with my sails and the sun with my open face.

I ignore the slim weight of my phone between the denim of my back pocket. I press one boot into the grass, after the other, and the other, until my thoughts find their way into the essay I have been trying to write.

AUCHINLECK, AYRSHIRE.

9.15 A.M.

A mist hangs in the long fields, slung low over the tussocks.

There is a fine dew silvering the mown lines along the driveway's curve, like the pewter sheen of a jackdaw's cape. There is bright sky in all the puddles. The bluetits are busy. The treeline's shape warps as you move your head, leaning closer to the view behind the old, rippled windowpane. Leaves are corroding in the damp October air.

You know that somewhere in amongst those trees, roots grasp the skeleton of a long-lost home. Stone sinks into its soft pine-needle bed. Stone lies angular and velvety. Stone, arranged by careful hands into a vaulted arch, holds up four hundred accumulated years of forest floor. Two trees grow tall from clutched foundations; taller than the last remaining chimney breast, spreading branches where heavy roofs once hung. It is a shaded cathedral of bark and masonry, creaking and confetti-blown by the gathering autumn wind.

COLLINS
ENGLISH GEM

'Herrings!' my mum exclaims.

'Yep,' I say. 'Specifically herrings.'

According to a small section at the back of the *Collins English Gem* (1963 edition), there are six separate units dedicated to the sole purpose of quantifying herrings. No separate category is given to the measuring of herrings, as it is to the measuring of medicines or paper, but scattered in amongst 'chests' of cloves and 'chaldrons' of coal, are various names for specific quantities of herrings. They pop up so frequently you can't help but wonder if herrings have a history of being traded like money. 'How much do you think your goat is worth?' 'Oh, I don't know, about a long hundred of herrings.'

'I think herrings were very important to a lot of people, you know.' Mum's voice is earnest, fizzing through the phone, and I know she's sharing my enthusiasm in these linguistic discoveries.

A 'long hundred of herrings' is equivalent to '132 herrings' or 'thirty-three warps'. And a 'warp', should you need to know, is exactly four herrings. To my great delight, I also discover that 'ten hundred' refers to exactly 1,320 herrings, while a 'last of herrings' numbers 13,200. Alternatively, you may prefer to measure your herrings by the gallon, and so it would be useful to note that thirty-seven-and-a-half gallons make up a 'cran of herrings', and that in Scotland, a barrel of cured herrings (for they must be cured, and they must be in Scotland), is equivalent to exactly twenty-six-and-two-thirds of a gallon.

'*Especially* the Scots,' Mum says. 'They would have people posted in lookout towers on the cliffs, when the herrings were meant to be coming.'

I laugh, creaking the back of my desk chair, trying to visualise this claim.

'They could see them coming in, at the right time of year, arriving in huge numbers. Then they'd ring a bell or something.'

When I was about thirteen, my mum gave me her old pocket dictionary. It is a slim, wallet-sized book, with round corners bending softly around the fraying tissue paper pages. I love this type of page, the kind that quivers as it turns, like the tiny New Testaments handed out in a special assembly in primary school. The words show backwards through each translucent sheet.

This dictionary of Mum's is covered in a papery blue plastic, cross-hatched to imitate something like leather. Creases web its surface, like lines in the skin of an old palm. In simple italic lettering, stamped in cracking silver, the top right corner reads:

Collins
English Gem
Dictionary

'I used to keep it in my leather satchel,' she's told me. 'It fitted perfectly in a pocket in the front.' The dictionary was essential during her secondary school years, answering questions she couldn't answer with the internet.

I didn't make much practical use of this book, assuming rightly that my shiny *Pocket Oxford Dictionary and Thesaurus* was more up to date. It is a laminated wedge of information, as thick as it is wide and certainly not able to fit in any pocket I own. It has a sleek, graphic cover and sturdy pages, that smelled, for years, like the peppermint bath bomb it had been next to in my Christmas stocking. It was my chosen companion as I read *Jane Eyre* for the first time, and *Wuthering Heights* after that.

The *Collins Gem* – opened only for the moreish crinkle of its bible-thin pages – was for numerous years tucked safely into a drawer. The same drawer held a stack of unfinished diaries, old postcards, some Olbas Oil and a Golden Virginia tobacco tin – the size of a pack of cards – hiding coins and badges and a special curl of tree bark. The tin had belonged to my grandad, a cheerful toolmaker and life-long smoker whose lungs finally wore out not long before I discovered Charlotte Brontë.

There are more of these slim green tins in Mum's sewing drawers, rattling with spare bobbins and tailor's chalk.

Now, in my twenties, and with an endless supply of spellings and synonyms in my pocket smartphone, I find myself opening the small, blue *Gem* once more. It's about 9.45 p.m., and I've managed to finish my day early enough for a reading session. I'm chipping away at a healthy to-be-read stack beside my bed, and Andrew is about fifty pages into *Jane Eyre*. I'm thrilled that he's finally got around to reading it, and quite jealous that he gets to do it for the first time.

'Penurious,' he says suddenly. 'What's that?' Refreshingly, neither of our phones are near, but next to my pile of books is Mum's dictionary, the *Oxford Pocket* having been mislaid in our most recent move. So we use it. And it feels so snug and comfortable between my fingers as they flick the fragile pages: 'Penurious: a. unwilling to spend; mean.'

Soon we're looking for weapons; obscure 'x' and 'z' words to keep in mind for the next Scrabble tournament: 'xylocarp';[5] 'zephyr'.[6] And then onto the next highest scoring: 'q'. Here I find my new favourite word – 'queachy (kwe'chi) a. yielding or trembling under the feet, as moist or boggy ground.' I work my way through this sweetie-shop of old and new, repeating the best of them a few times, shaping the sounds with relish.

Jane Eyre temporarily forgotten, we soon discover that, in addition to its wonderful selection of 'essential' words, their definitions short and efficient to the point of poetry, the old *Collins Gem* keeps one of its greatest gifts till last. At the back are a few pages set aside for what you might call 'useful information': The Longest Rivers, Highest Mountains, Important Events in British and Foreign History. But the best section are the two short pages titled: 'Miscellaneous Weights and Measures'.

Aside from the herrings, I learn some brilliant ways to talk about certain foods: a hogshead of sugar, a peck of flour, a bushel of barley and a barrel of butter (which is, of course, equal to four firkins). I learn the phrase 'a pig of ballast' – one I must have repeated at least fifteen times since, despite knowing that I'll never have a use for it.

---

5. (zi'lo-karp) n. hard, woody, fruit. – xylocarp'ous a. having fruit that becomes hard or woody.
6. (zef'ir) n. the west wind; gentle breeze; fine woollen fabric.

I learn that a truss of hay means different weights depending on whether you're referring to new hay, old hay or straw (makes sense), and that you must specify whether a bale of cotton is 'Egyptian', 'Indian' or 'USA', because each refer to quite different quantities. I also now know that a pipe of port is 115 gallons of the stuff – another lovely phrase which, to my great disappointment, I'm sure I will never need.

Even outside of the 'Miscellaneous' section, there are some excellent weights and measures to be learned. Under 'Apothecaries' Weight' I discover that twenty grains equate to one 'scruple', which leads to the delicious realisation that this here is the origin of the word 'scrupulous'. A scruple!

Under 'Paper Measure', I discover that, smaller than the well-known *ream* of paper, is the *quire*. Twenty-four sheets make up a quire, and twenty quires make up a ream. Two of these reams make a bundle, and ten reams equal a bale. A printer's ream, however, is twenty-one-and-a-half quires of paper. Like a baker's dozen, it's these fantastically inconvenient idiosyncrasies in so many of our old ways that I love stumbling upon so much.

I should add that, according to our trusty *English Gem*: 'In a ream of paper there are two outside or damaged quires. An outside quire of paper contains only 20 sheets.' Of course it does!

This little blue dictionary makes me think about the poetry that is passed down, hidden amongst our daily language, or sometimes tucked away in places it might be forgotten or lost. Rhymes and turns of phrases are handed over but their roots are pulled out of the ground they came from. We use our words without thinking – but their sound can hold generations of meaning, of life and use.

Finally, before the book expires in conversion tables and chemical symbols, there is one polite section slotted in, as if to fill a gap:

HOW TO TELL THE DAYS
IN EACH MONTH
Days in the Month
30 days have September,
April, June and November;
All the rest have 31,
Excepting February alone,
Which has but 28 days clear,
And 29 in each leap year.

There is a quiet childishness to this final offering. I am transported back to babbling primary school classes, hearing a chorus of voices recite the useful rhyme, which always, every time, trail off into a mishmash of unsure versions at the end – trying to explain the awkward February bit. Even the teachers didn't know how it went. I spent my life – until now – unsatisfied with a chant that was so useful, and yet so stumbling and forgettable at the end. The sight of this final section warms my heart for reasons I can't quite measure or weigh.

'You know, I think that was my grandfather's before it was mine,' Mum says on the phone, 'your great-grandad. He used to keep it by him when he read, to look up words if he didn't know the meaning.'

In the same conversation, I find out that when my mum was a child, her dad – my grandad – gave her *Jane Eyre* for Christmas.

'It was my first grown-up book. It had a red cover with gold embossed writing and gold edges to the pages. The paper was very thin and the print small, but I loved it.

'It felt very special to own it myself. There weren't so many books in the house,' she says, 'but we had the public library.'

She tells me that almost every week, her dad would take her to the local library in Swindon, where she and her sister could choose a book and take it home. I think of our regular excursions to Penarth Library, how familiar that concrete ramp is in my mind, the railing under my small fingers, the brightly painted walls in the stairwell, the bean bags in the picture-book room…cosy and cave-like, full of stories.

From these working-class men, my mum inherited a permanent reading habit – and so did I. Like Mum, *Jane Eyre* was my first classic. Like Grandad, I love to read, to take out books from the library – though I didn't know we had this in common, not until after he was gone.

And like my great-grandad, I now keep this tiny dictionary next to me as I wade into new territories. I wonder if he ever flipped to those back pages, marvelled over the 'Miscellaneous Weights and Measures'. Or, being from a previous world, if he knew many of them already, and saw no need to question the age-old, herring-counting ways.

'You're probably right,' she says. 'They probably were like currency, once upon a time.'

I have to go, and I say goodbye just as Mum is googling the history of herring trading.

'I think they might be the same as kippers…'

The next time I'm able to visit home, I ask Mum about Grandad's toolbox. I remember, not long after he died, seeing a heavy wooden chest in our kitchen, dusty and fronted with a mosaic of small drawers.

We find it sitting in her garden shed still coated with the same dust. 'I think it has woodworm,' she admits. 'Though I do mean to sort it out.'

I spend the next few days, with the help of both my parents, restoring Grandad's toolbox in the garden. I clean it, treat it with special chemicals to stop the woodworm, sand it all down – every edge – until my fingernails are scratched ragged from the sandpaper. I take out the remaining hinge bracket, from when it once had a pull-down front panel, and try to level the three surviving corner feet.

Then, instead of transforming the toolbox with the fashionable teal furniture paint I bought, I clean it again and use some teak oil to bring the dark chestnut colour back into the wood. I watch all the marks and nicks and the ring stain on its top become part of the pattern of the chest. I polish each of the chocolately, Bakelite drawer knobs, then I leave it out to dry in the sun. I think how beautiful it looks, my grandad's toolbox, with all its use and years soaked into the grain.

A year later, Nanny, my mum's mother, is very ill in hospital. I find out that when she and my grandad moved from Swindon – when I was very little, to be nearer to their grandchildren – my Nanny took to swimming in the sea at Barry Island.

'She loved to go in the sea,' Mum tells me, and the flicker of a memory arrives. A zebra-print swimsuit and metal fold-out deckchairs. The image tugs on something in my chest. All these things I share with those who went before me; everything that's passed along, folded away, kept safe, forgotten.

Grandad's box sits now in my study. Its drawers are lined with wallpaper and filled with all my tools: pencils, pens, stapler, hole punch, ink cartridges and paper clips. The upright nook on the left-hand side – likely made for some removable part that's long-since gone – now houses a row of notebooks and scrap paper. And the uppermost drawer in the right-hand corner, one of the small, square, shallow ones, holds an old blue conversion book for calculating measurements. Well-thumbed and full of numbers, this pamphlet was in the toolbox when I inherited it.

I slide open the drawer below this one and take out an old blue dictionary with tissue-paper pages. I go over to my desk and sit back down, shuffling the chair under as my thumbs fan tiny words out into the room.

MARSKE-BY-THE-SEA.

4.50 P.M.

The tide has come back in again, all the way, pushing shells and pebbles up the sand like pennies in an arcade game.

The wind is sweeping: long rushing gusts of sea-chilled air. Turbines spin fast, their blades rotating out of sync. Neat rows on the horizon.

Thumbprints of seaweed and ocean shrapnel have gathered along the shoreline. Their crescents bank-up foam; salty lather accumulated from each spent wave. Once in a while there is a breakaway: a flurry of snow, clinging froth succumbed to the gale, skimming across the sand in shrinking crumbs – each time chased frantically by dogs off leads, all delighted with the game.

There is strange light buried in the churning sky. Beach stretches on for miles both ways, stretching on to other towns with different weather. Darker clouds, headlands smeared behind slanted rainfall.

The sea charges in towards the dunes. It reaches twice a day for the ribboning coastal road; for the soft edge of Yorkshire.

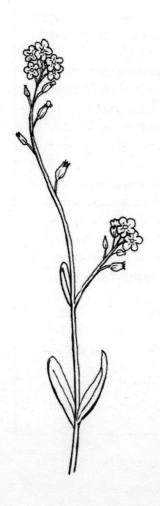

THE NATURE OF CHANGE

Fire

*Nothing in nature is forever…Gatherings of species
in time and space may give the illusion of stability,
but these communities can only last as long as the
conditions that help create them persist.*

Thomas Halliday,
Otherlands: A World in the Making

OL21: SE.049.119 It is March 2022, and the morning is
bright and bafflingly warm. I arrive at the National Trust
carpark early, having set an unusual Saturday alarm and left
home before anyone else had stirred on the street.

I climb out of the car and open the boot, sitting on its edge as I swap my plimsolls for walking boots. The carpark is already filling with families and their dogs. Marsden is out in full colour and it's only breakfast time. It's a far cry from when we first found the place, back in the autumn of 2020.

I close my rucksack, lock the car and walk down to the information centre where I've been told to meet. There are a few people there already, adding or removing layers, tightening laces and rummaging in bags. Cheerful words are exchanged, and I join them without further introduction. The weather, the sun, night shifts and Raynaud's. I listen and nod while I eat my banana. A jar is passed around: contributions towards the work that the National Trust does here. We wait as more walkers merge politely into the circle of boots.

Paul arrives. He is a small, bespectacled, sixty-something man, with a weather-worn bucket hat and trousers tucked sensibly into his socks. He is wearing an impressive number of layers for this spring warmth, but none of us will see him remove a single one throughout the day. Paul has been a volunteer for thirty years, it turns out, and has been leading this Ten Reservoir Walk for almost as many.

He greets a few familiar faces, then blows his nose on a cotton handkerchief, clears his throat, and addresses the group.

'Hello, everyone. Now, as you might already know, we've had some fires this week.'

I had caught wind, just the night before, that there had been another wildfire on the moor. The timing was farcical. I had planned to join this walk for research weeks ago: I've been thinking deeply for many months about change and recovery, and though we no longer live in this old industrial part of Yorkshire, I want to know more about the moorland landscape that, a year ago, had been our unexpected haven. I was tempted back by its history...and by its particular habit of catching fire.

Paul sniffs and continues: 'I've been up and it's no longer smouldering, but it is very dusty and dirty. We won't be taking one of the paths. I think we'll go up to the road and along, which will add about a mile.'

'That makes it a fifteen-mile walk, not a fourteen-mile one,' a daughter beside me whispers to her mother.

Another member of staff, the park ranger, gives the usual health-and-safety speech, and cheeriness flickers back into the circle. A few late arrivals add their donations to the jar, straps are tightened, buckles clicked, and then we're off – straight up the hill and out of the village, panting introductions, warming up stiff ankles, laughing off any nervousness about the many miles ahead.

The first climb is apparently one of the toughest, so I try not to take my breathlessness too seriously. I've grown up hiking hills and mountains back in Wales, I've got all my Duke of Edinburgh certificates, but I feel very out of practice. I've never signed up for an expedition like this before. I feel flushed with the achievement of having gotten myself here, and with the sudden question in my mind of how one is supposed to stop for a wild wee when they are marching amongst a group of strangers.

We are above the houses and shedding layers of fleece already. A train of scouts storm past us, hurrying with beginners' optimism on their annual walking challenge. I'm told there's a prize for the fastest team.

At the end of the green-tunnelled path, I mount a stile which marks the gateway to the moor tops. I pause.

Ahead of me, black tussocks shroud the hilltop, their edges crumbling to soot in the wind.

The first time I met the Marsden Moors, they were damp and rusting. The late October air was full of rain, the bracken skeletal and auburn, and the paths slick with clay. Our boots barely held us to the hill. Andrew and I followed our route in awe, skirting around valleys that filled us with relief.

We had arrived in Huddersfield a month earlier, the same week that it entered what would be its longest lockdown yet. With no knowledge of the area and no friends nearby, we were on our own. The two of us spent those first weeks looking for furniture online, working from mobile hotspots, and fitting ourselves into the house we had picked from a few dim photos and a video tour. Now, finally, we could breathe. We had found a place of escape within the strict limits of our permitted territory, and it was vast.

The Wessenden Valley, the south part of the wider Marsden Moors, was our chosen refuge. A finger poking a quiet backdoor into the Dark Peaks, it straddles the awkward point where three different OS Maps meet: Peak District (OL1), South Pennines (OL21) and Bradford & Huddersfield (288). The valley cradles three Victorian reservoirs and meanders down into the old industrial cluster of Marsden. But, if you venture into its folds, cross the shallow river and climb up onto its wily edges, you see the land at large.

We stumbled upon this view on our second visit to the moors. Having walked around the deeper creases of the west side of the valley – our path following the curves cut by tributaries – we reached the fork where our green dotted line left the map we had brought and went west. We decided to save that path for another day, so began our descent down to the familiar reservoirs that would guide us back towards our car. The hill was steep, but its path rocked us patiently from side to side, navigating loose rubble and wiry shrubs. It wasn't until almost halfway down, when we waited on a bend for a puffing pair to pass us safely, that I lifted my eyes from my feet.

The valley was in full colour. All the bracken was at its roughest auburn. The shallow river winding its silvery way between the hillsides was bordered in vibrant green.

The white sky hung soft and low, curtaining off the distant streets and junctions and tightly sealed buildings we were so glad to be out of. There are more breathtaking, and certainly more unusual views in the British Isles, but there is a special balance and beauty to this one, caught from the twist of a steep footpath. I took a photo and have taken one from the same spot each time we have visited since; the land laid out in different seasons, the same contours under different shades of weathered light. A private record of this place and how it changed for us. And, while we needed it, how it didn't change at all.

When harder frosts arrived, we ventured out, crunching through a light snowfall that had melted back in town. It sharpened the hills, as if a stick of white chalk had been dragged across their textured surface. The setting sun, as we came back to the lowest lake, bled pastel pinks into its glossy surface, sending the whole vista into something like an oil painting.

In the coldest week of winter, February 2021, the pair of us jingled up the access track and into the buried valley, kicking through a shingle of shattered ice – hard crystal rubble from the pond-sized potholes. Clay-stained icicles hung like organ pipes from path-side rock faces. That day, going up and over the top was a bold commitment. There were wind chills well below minus ten, and a colourless tundra in all directions. It was the best day we'd had in weeks.

Fifteen minutes' drive followed by an hour's walk from our small cream-carpeted rental, this view became our anchor. It beckoned us from the manic circuit board of weekdays among the concrete. Regardless of the latest theories, arguments, outrages and catastrophes, this valley continued on its way – rolling quietly, reliably, through the seasons.

OL21: SE.041.135 I walk quietly in the gap between the hikers at the front and the ramblers at the back. I rest my eyes on the path we follow through the aftermath – a ribbon of survival cutting through the middle, too compacted and worn to have offered any fuel.

Moorland fires are not uncommon around Marsden, but they are becoming disturbingly frequent. Barbeques and campfires are entirely banned across the National Trust's managed estate here, but that doesn't stop the occasional fool – perhaps a cigarette smoker or a kid with a firework – from setting the landscape alight. Here a fire spreads quickly, and the ancient peat can smoke for weeks.

Walking between two expanses of char, I want to say something. To ease it all into acknowledgement, to pin my feelings down with language before they drift off with the dust and settle somewhere else. But I don't know any of the people I've come here with; none of their names or voices. The questions I want to ask the park ranger, the volunteers, and Paul, carousel themselves around my mind. The ash glitters like coal dust in the high sun, and I walk on.

After the snow, the long winter within walls, and with the heather bleached brown by the cold, Andrew and I were waiting eagerly for the colour of spring. But just as the brightest greens made ready to unfurl, the whole scene changed. The view from our favourite path in April 2021, showed a valley divided.

At first, approaching from a distance, we weren't sure if the hill had always looked this dark…Was it the withered heather exposing the peat after winter? Was the sky hanging more heavily today? But the closer we got, the blacker it became, until finally a sadness settled onto me that felt a bit like grief.

The land was bruised, one side black as if deep in a storm cloud's shadow. The ripple at the foot of its slope slotted into the opposite side of the valley like two mismatched pieces of a puzzle. Its opposite was green and sprouting from every pore. The stark contrast snaked down and away from us, down into the water pooled at the foot of the drained-dry moorlands.

This was the landscape we depended on for its wilderness and permanence. Each month it changed, but there's a comfort in the predictability of such a cycle, knowing that those same turns – be they late or early – come around like clockwork every year. Like the sun rising, or the moon waxing. Such a sudden and extreme transformation, the scorching of the earth for miles around, was a shock.

Seldom are we faced with the irreversible. We've become so used to being able to hit the 'undo' button, to wipe things clean, to fix whatever it is we've broken. Up on the mule track, the stepping stones were dusted with ash, and smoke was still in the air. We didn't know what words to use, and fell quiet, like unsure mourners at the funeral of a recent acquaintance. It smelled hot. It smelled like cinder and frustration.

'You won't believe how soon it will spring back to life,' my dad reassured me over the phone. 'Next time you visit, it will be green again.'

I wasn't so sure. It seemed like spring had been cancelled – stopped in its tracks – and I couldn't see where it would go from there.

But, as promised, the barrenness dissolved. A few weeks later we returned and found life growing in all directions. Summer was arriving, like it always does. This time I was shocked, not by the distress of change, but by the unstoppable elasticity of it. Change as resistance. It looked as though Marsden Moors had reacted to our carelessness with undeterred industry. Adapt – and thrive.

That spring, as the weather warmed, we were being herded onto a 'road map' out of restricted living. After a

long string of inconsistencies things were changing again.
I was trying to find a meaning for the word 'recovery' that
made sense to me now. There were changes I hadn't yet
been able to name, and which I was beginning to feel might
not be so easily reversed.

I was also nurturing a quiet anger over the rapid and
devastating impact humans have had on natural landscapes
– feeding it with books like Annie Proulx's *Barkskins* and
The Overstory by Richard Powers, and articles which
spoke of ecological amnesia: 'You think the coral reefs are
depleting now? Just look at what they *used* to be.'

I already knew how deeply we can hurt our surroundings;
Covid-19 had first entered the news amongst a surge
of footage of the wildfires in Australia. I had seen those
pictures, understood the consequences of lost habitats, but I
hadn't *felt* it before. With the fresh smell of moorland smoke
in my nostrils and a sense of injustice in my heart, I was
noticing it everywhere.

Only a few months later, following a lucky visit to our local
vaccine centre in Huddersfield, we seized an unexpected
opportunity and crossed the Atlantic. With Andrew's father
unwell and so much time spent unable to travel, we stayed
for two months in Ontario; working remotely, and doing
what we could to enjoy Canada's slow shift back into gear.

As the high summer began to soften and our time
remaining shrank, we borrowed Andrew's parents' car and
drove out of the city to Algonquin Provincial Park.

There is a close and evident history of logging in
Algonquin. The trails we walked were studded with
reminders of the large-scale destruction of such places
across the evergreen blanket of North America. Algonquin
seemed like an island of verdant survival in what was now
a tapestry of agriculture, young shrubland, and city. But

even there, in what seemed like perfect wilderness, much was missing.

Far from our recovering English hills, the breeze that had been wafting white clouds overhead was gone, and early evening sunlight filtered weakly into the cool shade. We were on a path that was winding but well-trodden. Andrew and I were looking for markers: little plastic discs nailed into thick bark, to tell us which trees we were standing beneath, and where on the hand-drawn map we had paused.

Most of the trees we saw in Algonquin were young by woodland standards: offspring, 'second stand', the generation that came after all the clearance. But the trail we had come to wrapped around a small colony of old growth White Pines. The tallest stood because of the bowed sweep of their trunks that rendered them 'useless'. The rest were there because of their particular age: when the loggers arrived on this hillside in the 1880s, these pines were too spindly to bother with, having been stunted in their growth by older, towering trees that have all since been felled, stripped and dragged away to shipyards. With those giants gone, these young pines could take their place in the sun, accelerating into the impressive heights they are today.[7]

Only a small handful of old-growth pines remain in Algonquin Park, and those odd few, though protected fiercely, are likely to reach their natural end within the next century. It seems that White Pine, in particular, only grow against the odds, and that though they dominated this landscape not so long ago, the species is destined to struggle into obscurity here.

---

7. I gleaned most of this knowledge from a wonderful booklet which accompanied the trail: information carefully gathered by The Friends of Algonquin Park, and which transformed our surroundings into a living museum.

I'm told that a White Pine can grow anywhere once it's gotten started, but that getting started is the hard part. Dead leaves, bigger plants, munching mouths – all are enough to scupper a young shoot's efforts to reach daylight. So why were their sweeping trunks towering over this slope? The area has the ideal conditions for sugar maples, whose spreading leaves should have thwarted any attempts for pine saplings to make it through those difficult first years. But the magnificent White Pine can sow its seeds successfully in one very particular circumstance: when the rest of the forest is in flames.

Tree rings, like ice cores, are archives of change, and can be read like history books. Count the rings from the oldest trunks in this crop, and you'll know that a forest fire took hold here in the year 1790.

It would have been the perfect fire: just the right intensity and at just the right time. Too gentle, and the ground wouldn't be cleared enough to expose that patient soil. Too early, and the nearby pines would not be ready to shed their fruit before other plants returned en masse. Too ferocious, like some of the fire storms we see swirling on our television screens today, and there would be nothing left at all.

Standing among the trees that evening, I imagined the heat that birthed them. In *Barkskins* I had read about the careless outbreaks that swept through miles of precious lumber, but this fire would have happened before the European invasion reached these woods. This perfect fire would have been sparked by a lightning bolt, striking a tree in the rumbling night, choosing just the right moment to take hold.

For trees like this, wildfires are a natural cycle, happening once in a thundery blue moon; relied upon every few hundred years to encourage the next generation of growth. Of course, wildfires now can mean something quite different. Vicious tornadoes kindled in the dusty height of summer droughts, tearing wide corridors of unexpected destruction through already weakened habitats. But this story of the White Pines in Ontario nevertheless made me think of the green unfurling so quickly from the black at home. The wildflowers thriving in the mineral ash; the phoenix plants profiting gratefully from the sudden loss of their predecessors.

I stood at the base of a trunk, almost as wide as our terraced house, soaking my skin in its cool shade. It smelled like damp needles and tea leaves.

Even when the last of the old pines fall in their protected forests, research suggests that the main ecosystems relying on the giants can still thrive in younger, second-stand forests. The whole chain marches on, taking change in its stride, battling – and beating – far more obstacles every season than the loss of the White Pines.

OL21: SE.039.146 Before long, we are out of the blackened landscape and onto the road that Paul has designated for our detour. Once in a while, a shout comes from the back of the group and we all peel to the verge as a 4x4 rockets past at eighty miles an hour, relishing this unsupervised open straight. I wish we were walking through the wasteland again.

I swing an ankle over a stile. The grass underfoot is unburned, but loose and dead, bedding the trail like hay in a rabbit hutch. It's a sea of bone-dry kindling. Give it one glowing stub, or, as someone mutters, even just the midday sun through an empty plastic bottle.

Eventually, I catch up with Paul's relentless pace at the front. I ask him a few questions about the burning of Marsden Moors, searching hopefully for more evidence that nature could withstand our mistakes. He tells me about millennium grass.

'You're right that it does recover quickly, but it's not always the same plants that were there before which are growing back.'

Paul tells me that the ash of wildfires causes the soil to become more acidic, which some plants enjoy more than others.

'The more fires we have, the more this grass takes over. And then we're more likely to have another fire...It's a vicious cycle.'

The wetter the moors are, the safer they are. Millennium grass, it turns out, is the thatch we have been walking over much of the morning. Not only is it rubbish at helping the earth to hold rainwater, but it also dries into swathes of fire fodder.

I have read about the work the National Trust are doing to try to bring more sphagnum moss back to the landscape, with lots of volunteers helping to plant plugs of this spongy friend every winter, all over the hills.

'We've also been building leaky dams in strategic places,' says Paul. 'They slow down the water running off the moors, so that it can soak in and be retained.'

This is all part of a process of 're-wetting' Marsden, which isn't just about preventing fires, but reducing floods, too. If water runs straight off the hills and down the valleys, rivers are much more likely to burst their banks than if it filters through the system slowly, keeping everything damp and happy.

According to Paul, acidity has been an issue long before these bouts of wildfires. During the industrial revolution, clouds of pollution from Manchester would blow east and empty out over these hills as acid rain.

'Now that *really* affected the biodiversity. It's what we're still trying to fix with the work we're doing now.'

I admire the determination of these people in what must often feel like the impossible task: protecting peat, re-introducing species, encouraging reluctant mosses, battling invasive plants...But it strikes me that perhaps this – their mission to restore the landscape to what it was before – *is* the impossible task. The main question in my mind is: how do we know which 'before' is the right one?

I look out across the hills, and I think about the glacier sheets that pushed and shoved them into shape, about the trees that once spired the horizon, the unrecognisable beasts that grazed its unmarked territories. I think about the smog of the industrial revolution locked among the heather roots; the trees dragged away from their hillside in Ontario; the one spark flung from a cheap disposable barbecue, igniting the wind faster than anyone could stop it.

As we walk on, mulling through the sea of millennium grass, I think about the phrase that is being repeated, over and over: *return to normal*. Words I am beginning to understand as make-believe. The idea that we can 'return' to anything that has been archived by the turn of the Earth... and the very notion that 'normal' is something that can be chalked-out or stapled down.

'They used to drop fuel here you know,' says Paul. 'Kerosene...The aeroplanes would dump it all out before coming into land at Manchester. In case they crashed, I suppose. It was a safety thing.' He squints across the low green farmland below.

'No,' he says. 'These moors have not been treated well.'

Water

When viewed in deep time, things come alive that seemed inert. Ice breathes, rock has tides, mountains ebb and flow [...] We live on a restless earth.

Robert Macfarlane, *Underland*

OL21: SE.017.131 One of the reservoirs we are introduced to on our hike across the Marsden Moors holds seventy-one million gallons of water. It feeds the Huddersfield canals and sits in a basin rimmed by the high curve of that racing-track A road. Above March Haigh Reservoir is a high mound – March Hill – which Paul points to as he addresses the group.

'That there is where Neolithic folk would have come and camped. For hunting. It gave them a view of the land in all directions.' He fumbles to remember the details of this story which has ignited a few of the group's interest. 'They, er, they found ash, and flint chips, so they know they would have sat around a fire up there, whittling their arrows and such.'

Back then, the reservoir was not a reservoir. It was the running river that carved this bowl out, cushioned by long-lost trees. And before that, the view was of the glacier that left March Hill here in the first place.

The Marsden Moors are the product of constant, gradual, and occasionally abrupt change. But it feels strange to step back from what we think is most still – the ground beneath us – and see it as a moving thing. Mountains have risen and worn away, glaciers have bullied old surfaces into new contours, estuaries have cut through lands and created others. Our island holds the scars of tectonic change – plates shifting and scrunching until our great-grandfathers came, just a moment ago, to chart their shape and set it in ink.

As I walk, I try to step back far enough for the human footprint on this land to shrink to just a centimetre on the ruler. But even in that centimetre, so much has taken place. Each fraction holds so many lives; and each life so many different skies.

Two weeks ago, I was 10,973 metres above Newfoundland and Labrador, on a more recent, more sudden visit to family. Facemask pressed to the oval window, I watched white cliffs appear, rising up out of the shattered sea. Over the frozen mountains I saw the snail-trails of rivers, topaz in the thaw, winding towards the coast, and the occasional independent curl of an oxbow lake. A tight rivulet meander, destined for the same fate, reminded me of the arteries that wriggle water down a sandy beach. From so high, I felt I could release the stream from its writhing detour with one dig of a plastic trowel.

But elsewhere there are towns and cities built in the crook of a river bend. We plant our stakes in sites like these – build cathedrals, cafés and family homes – and we plan to stay put. We expect the river to do the same.

We give living land boundaries and expect it to stay within the lines. Neatly detailed maps with 'official' stamps trick us into thinking that what we see is correct, immovable, *normal*.

I wondered how long, in the uninhabited valleys of Newfoundland with no stakes planted or reinforcing concrete poured, it would take for that rushing river bend to become a placid crescent lake.

We leave March Haigh and cut out across the heather. With the hollow knock of stone slabs beneath my boots, the sunken stone bridges and horizon cobbled brown under the bright sun, it's hard to accept that this place has ever been any other way.

I clunk along the same pack-horse path that my great, greater and even greater grandmothers might have, carrying worries and water and lunch, and looking out across the same steep valley sides. Only those women would not have lifted their eyes to the wide open blue and seen it cross-hatched with contrails.

OL1: SE.058.089 By mid-afternoon, we are dipping down into the Wessenden Valley – my familiar territory – and skirting along a straight, brick-sloped water's edge. The Wessenden Reservoir is the highest pearl on this valley's string, and holds 107 million gallons of rain, benevolently feeding the reservoirs below, and then the towns and canal ways beyond.

Crossing the dam in the winter means bracing the wind that brushes off the surface of the black waters. There is no colourful life frilling around this reservoir's edges, no gentle shallows, just the neat masonry of the slope that breaks its ice-blown ripples.

Today, however, the breeze is gentle and sleeves are rolled. Tame fallow deer are grazing in their usual field beside the old lodge. The pheasants are grazing, too, pecking absent-mindedly. They trim the green-carpeted bank that keeps all that water up there, so high above the houses.

We reach the other side, cross the main track, and pause at the foot of our next climb. This path is new – it appeared one winter weekend, after lots of sliding mud, and likely thanks to a gang of mountain bikes that decided to take a shortcut. Bikes aren't allowed on the moors, to keep erosion to a minimum and protect the breeding wildlife. Mike, the park ranger hiking with us, has been telling two-wheeled blokes off with decreasing patience all afternoon. Two were on motorbikes, spluttering up tracks that had clearly seen the same abuse before. He called the police for that pair.

Our guides tell us that they use this unofficial path out of the valley regularly now, though it tends to be like ripping off a plaster. Straight up, no meanders, until we hit the old highway on top. The group readies itself: boots tightened; sleeves knotted around waists. And then we march.

If you were to fly on from Newfoundland and Labrador, curving south and westward, you would reach a place called The Thousand Islands. There is a lacy bulge in the St Lawrence as it skims Canada's border with the US, and then meets, mouth wide, the mighty Lake Ontario. That stretch of river is scattered with a total of 1,864 islands – contrary to its modest but memorable name – clustering in every size and shape to create a bewildering archipelago. Some peep just above the blue-green waters, exposing enough dry land for a holiday home to be cemented onto it. Others are dense with tree shade, sending jetties into the sun. Some are so small they consist of just a rocky mound and a single sapling: enough, according to the mysterious powers who decide these things, for it to be classified as one of those 1,864 islands.

We went to Ganonoque, 'the gateway to the 1000 islands', in the same summer that we found Algonquin. And it was these islands, after reeling from the wildfires and hiding from the daily news, which triggered an understanding of how tiny my idea of permanence really was.

Early on an August morning, with the sky burning blue and water already warm between our fingers, Andrew and I paddled out on a kayaking excursion. We were with a group of other curious visitors, though I was the only one coming from across borders. Canada was still only allowing citizens (Andrew) and, with enough paperwork, their partners (me), to enter the country. I was in quiet awe of a place I had known about only vaguely, as more fable than geography. It had been mentioned wistfully by my grandmother who, once upon a time, lived nearby for a while.

We twirled our double-ended paddles with growing confidence, meandering around the first few islands on our route. A few loops and I felt very glad we chose a guided trip – so many different edges make it difficult to keep hold of your orientation.

Some parts were very shallow, where an island's edges spread out just below the surface. Pieces of a boat wreck lay within a paddle's reach, planks and barrels verdant in the sunlight, weeds wavering around our passing kayaks.

I was trying to adjust my view of the place – to see the water as the thing linking all of these islands, instead of separating them. Even in the winter, when everything freezes over, and boats are swapped for sleds and skates. The dry ground was the thing we must skirt around.

I was busy turning the land inside out in my mind when we began to cross the main channel. This we needed to do swiftly and in a close group, because out in the open highway, we were in the potential course of large yachts and tour boats. As we paddled, our guide explained that this, where the water is suddenly dark and choppy, was the deepest part of the river, where the bed falls away at a cliff edge down below. This channel, if emptied out, would be comparable to the Grand Canyon.

The Thousand Islands were once an ancient lowland mountain range; crags and gorges cut deep into some of the oldest rock on the planet. We were floating on what was just the latest version of this landscape – flooded by water from the Great Lakes, via the St Lawrence 'Lowlands' (now 'River') following the last ice age, only about 10,000 years ago.

When I heard this, I marvelled. I imagined these brightly painted holiday homes teetering on hilltops, marooned from one another by the empty air. I looked around and tried to see these little islands for what they were: peaks, hiding the bulk of their mass beneath the placid surface. Like icebergs tipped with flags and deck chairs.

Since the Thousand Islands, I've been finding clues of transformation everywhere: amongst the windy pancake stacks of Yorkshire's Brimham Rocks, once flushed and grooved by silty river water, now perched high in the Dales; on our annual walk around a glacial valley in Bannau Brycheiniog, so recently moulded by the ice; and in books that tell me that even the Mediterranean Sea has recently been and gone, drained dry and filled again, while continents shift beyond any modern recognition, and then shift some more.

OL1: SE.058.089 Puffing and triumphant we arrive on the top of the ridge and look back to see the Wessenden Reservoir in shadow below. How brilliant that our human bodies, of all these ages, can get us up a hill like that. How they forge on when we need them to.

When everyone has caught their breath and glugged some water, we continue. This time we tread a flat, wide path that follows an old catchwater out of Wessenden, curling past Marsden and around the hills to the east. Though knees are sore and feet heavy, we feel the simmer of energy that comes with a journey's final leg.

Every kilometre or so, we pass a crumbling bridge leading onto the deep-tussocked moorlands to our right. I ask why so many crossings were built. Where were they leading? Who was up here that needed such sturdy access? I imagine a whole town hunched on the hill, moated by the catchwater and somehow vanished now without a trace. I'm told that the bridges were simply for the farmers to drive their livestock onto the windy moortops. Today, there's little to see, and most farms are gone – leaving only the husked stone ghosts of bridges leading nowhere.

This place is now its wildlife, its peat, and the ten reservoirs that feed the civilisation teeming at its feet. Marsden is being preserved, to the best of our ability, in a state of imagined permanence: functional, peaceful and familiar. The rivers have been stoppered to a trickle, slowing their excavation of the land, and the moors have been drained dry, though volunteers scrabble to restore some kind of 'normal' to their soils.

The last time I came here – before we left one temporary home for another, moving full of the usual hope from West to North Yorkshire – I was hesitating on the edge of something I didn't feel ready for. I was tired of change, had grown comfortable with isolation, was afraid of things I used to do with ease, and even more afraid that this was as far as the new normal could take me. My anxieties weren't nameable or obvious, but they were there, and what I couldn't explain, I couldn't fix.

I felt unready for the shift into a post-pandemic era. I faced another new place that I must turn into my home. In trying to equip myself for this next wave of change, I searched desperately in nature for some evidence that change could be resisted, undone, recovered from. And though the bigger picture tells a different story – the graphs and reports and international conferences – my small findings showed me that recovery happens, yes…but it does not mean restoration.

We begin our descent back down towards the village, heading for the low canal that will lead us to our cars. Conversation moves to plans for the evening, the week, the blooming spring. We funnel down a rocky footpath that squeezes between old stone walls, running down the side of a short row of houses. A dog runs out to bark us over the stile, and laundry shivers on a rotary line. I realise that it's almost exactly two years to the day since we first plunged into a national lockdown.

It's true that there are familiar shoots of green unfurling now, and brighter blooms will be budding soon, too. But this is not the same landscape that it was last year, or the year before. Some things are perennial, but their leaves are new each time they emerge, growing glossy from the mulch of their predecessors.

Change, like time, is not reversible. Places like Marsden are not so much rocks to cling to when it sweeps around us. They are more like rivers. Life giving, adaptable, and always, for as long as they flow, moving forwards.

Hikers peel off as we reach Marsden. I thank Paul, Mike, and the other volunteers, wishing them no further wildfires, and we part ways. I climb into the driver's seat, tired and pleased, ready to go home. I drive east, away from the moors, from Marsden and Huddersfield, deep in the gathering of everything I have felt and thought over these past two years of change.

WEST BLOCKHOUSE, CLEDDAU ESTUARY.

JUST AFTER 10 P.M.

A gentle thunderclap of breaking waves. White foam glowing, as if under UV light. The intermittent blink of green and red buoys, strung carefully between the headlands. The twinkling crown of the oil refinery at Pembroke Dock: a rubble of jewels on the opposite shore, climbing into spires towards the dim stars, like ivy over ruins.

You imagine dark fins and whiskered faces, wondering where they might be now. The fish swimming safely in the dark. The gulls huddled in crannies you don't know about.

Behind you, the reliable, revolving flash of light. Under your knuckles, the metal rail, knobbled under a glossed layer of recent paint. The rocks below give themselves away, casting sharp shadows from the wash of an almost full moon.

You could read the pages of a book under this moon. Everything is sepia; the grass bleached, the dark sea silver-plated, reversing the whole scene's shadows like a negative photo reel.

TO MAKE
THE PERFECT
GRAVY

You both gasp. You are balanced in the door frame, and she is frozen, feet planted firmly in the tundra on the kitchen tiles.

Shhh— she begins, and you think, *this is it.*

Shhh— this is bad enough for her to say the word she wants to say but always replaces with…

Sugar!

Your mother's hands whip to her sides.

You laugh. You are small but you see the perfection in the moment. *Exactly!* you trumpet.

You think about all the times you tried to find some sensible connection to the words adults choose when things go wrong. You feel as though you have just seen the planets align.

But you do not think about fetching the dustpan. Nor do you consider the butter, already softened, which waits patiently on the side, never to be combined with the half kilo of caster sugar that just hit the kitchen floor.

You sit at the second largest of the nesting tables in the centre of the living room. You have the curved glass screen all to yourself. You have your bowl of Heinz spaghetti hoops. You have your buttered squares of toast. This is your time: it's been a busy morning at nursery and now you're ready for the Tweenies.

Asta la pasta, baby! you shout, as your socks skid down the hallway.

You take your designated place. You smell the tang of rich tomato. You watch the bouncy, steaming tendrils lower and curl into your bowl.

These butter-yellow plate-bowls, with safe, deep sides and painted blue rims.

You grin as a shovel of glistening sauce is deposited onto the heap.

You kneel up on the chair and reach urgently for the grated cheese.

It's your attempt that makes it into the family history books. Pizzas from scratch: one evening, with all of you coaxed into the kitchen together. Each of you rolls and stretches out your allotted podge of dough. You spread your sauce, sprinkle your cheese, press on pieces of ham and pepper and maybe one or two bits of mushroom. Then, a little more cheese.

Four mini pizzas go into the hot, whirring oven. Door shut and timer set. You watch through the browning glass as the rounds begin to puff, edges bubble. You lose patience and go away to some other distraction, coming back ten minutes later to the cackles of your siblings. *Look! Look at Katy's one!*

Exactly half of the pizza has lifted to a perfect vertical. Your dinner has a 90-degree angle, and for a flicker you are furious: why yours? *A failure*, you think. But then your young ears begin to process the laughter around you, and you understand that you can turn this into a triumph. This is a skill you will hone over the years, as the veritable runt of the litter.

Assembled around the table, each paired with their handmade pizzas, you seize your cutlery and tuck proudly into what will henceforth be known by all as The Sofa Pizza.

The chairs have polished eggs, one crowning each top corner of their wooden backs. Like bed knobs – perfect for hanging cardigans, aprons, the loop on the oven gloves. The seats are covered in thick flowered oil cloth that your mum has stapled neatly to their undersides.

Once upon a time you would stand on the chair, clutching these eggs, while your mum shuffled it in against the cupboard door. Now you climb up with a cushion and kneel on the chair, climbing down again each time you need to relocate to a slightly different portion of the counter.

From up here you can mix, sprinkle, roll, dust, measure and whisk. You can rub dough between your fingers until your hands ache and the sandy crumbs in the bowl are joined by fistfuls of currants, to be transformed into hot and sugary Welsh cakes.

Eyes are all fixed to the glow, and you know what you have to do. This is your test: to prove that you are independent. You don't need to ask or interrupt or plead, you just need to do what they do on TV: go into the kitchen and *fix yourself a snack*.

To save dragging a chair over to the switch, you leave the lights off and move between the shadows cast from the hallway lamp. You find a slice of bread but cannot quite slot it into the toaster. Really, it's the same thing anyway, you think, and you go to the fridge for some jam. All the jars are in the heavens: heights you couldn't reach even with a chair. You think for a while. Then you find the ketchup bottle in the cupboard and squirt it onto the bread. (You skip the butter stage because it seems like a lot of effort that doesn't justify its result. Especially as you never could distribute it thin like Mum. The spongy bread just rolls and rips.)

You spread the sauce around to the edges, taking time to make an even layer, inspecting the corners in the gloom. You feel a determination now. Of course you can do this by yourself. You don't need to ask for help, or answers, or anything, in fact.

Next, you need a drink. You cannot reach the tap, so your options are limited. That's fine, because you always liked *just juice* the best, and wonder why it is only offered at breakfast time. So you pour the orange liquid into a cup, take up your plate, and trot back to the living room.

You might be vertically challenged, but you are self-sufficient.

You enter the ring of screen watchers and coolly take your seat. Someone asks you what you have. You explain. Laughter erupts. You can smell the slice of bread soaking sweet under your nose. You take a sip from your cup and are surprised to find that breakfast time *just juice* is not, in fact, the same thing as squash without water.

To celebrate the new allotment – the full-length strip of mud transferred to her name – you go together for a picnic after school. It is early July, and the hamper holds a warm roast chicken from the supermarket. You sit on a blanket on the grassy path, beside what will become the strawberry patch. The sun sits low on the roof of the local transformer station. Together, lips sticky and smiling, the pair of you survey this kingdom from your new vantage point: the rolled-out rug of the allotments, all colour and frill, fine green netting and bamboo wig-wams. A sunken bathtub sits at the head of every plot, filled to dunk the watering cans. Some are busy with their own ecosystems, reeds and tangled pond weed, a home-made wooden gangplank for the frogs.

You did it in blind frustration. It was reckless. You acted on greedy impulse and now you can feel it sitting hard and stony in your tummy. For years you'll remember that particular kind of guilt you felt, as you froze, stock still behind the muslin curtain. You could feel Dad's eyes look around the room and hear the plastic light switch flick – with a flinch – as he decided there was no one here. And now you're in the dark, hiding in the dining room, shame heating the roots of your hair as you finish the Penguin bar you stole from the cupboard.

The worst of it all was that she said *go on then, you can have one, I suppose.* After you emerged sheepish from your secret felony.

You nurse that guilt for a decade before you finally tell them about it. The time you thought that justice was the defiant consumption of a chocolate biscuit.

Fizzy blue and pink milkshake bottles. Nobbled razzles. Flying, melting saucers. Giant stick-in-your-teeth strawbs for two pence, a blue jelly dolphin for five. Yellow-bellied snakes that stretch long till they snap and hang limp from your teeth. Strawberry laces, lances, pencils. Different coloured crocodiles that have the perfect chew: two pence. A gummy pizza if you spend ten pence, or a box of chocolate cigarettes for twelve.

You watch as the girl behind the counter picks each item from the Tupperware and counts it into the paper bag. You mouth the numbers as she goes, knowing the sums, certain you have calculated right. Fifty pence exactly. Fifty pence: the official allowance. Because it's Saturday again, and Saturday is Sweetie Day.

Your shoes and bag are already history on the hallway tiles. The letter from school is in her hand and you've got the permission you need: to the cupboard. A packet of prawn cocktail crisps. An apple from the bowl – part of your agreement. A glass of orange squash. You creep past the already battled-out TV in the living room and go upstairs. You turn on the little grey box in their room. You settle on Mum's side of the bed, drink on coaster. *Arthur* has just finished, and the song is starting for *Mona the Vampire*. It's not long before you've opened out the empty crisp wrapper, nicking the seam with your teeth and carefully pulling it flat. You lick the last crumbs and flavouring from the silver plastic: wishing, as ever, that they would give just a couple more crisps in those frugal multi packets.

The Takeaway is a ceremony and you have graduated to its higher levels throughout the years. Once, an egg would be fried when the curry arrived, for you to enjoy atop your beans on toast. Then you began to have a taste of someone's korma, a tear of naan. Soon it was a chicken chat starter all to yourself, complete with greasy lettuce and warm lemon wedge.

Once, you would snatch the beginner chopsticks – a pair of giant plastic tweezers – from the terracotta pot of options. Now you can manage right down to your egg fried rice at the bottom of the bowl before resorting to a fork, and even then, a sticky nugget of impaled sweet and sour chicken can collect most of it, like a magnet in a box of pins.

The Takeaway is special before it even begins. You are always the one to volunteer to go with Dad to collect it. You enjoy riding in the front seat, no big siblings to usurp you. The pair of you weave the quiet evening roads. You are important, there is a mission to complete.

Familiar greetings from behind the bar. Your gracious acceptance of the little chocolate they never fail to offer, unwrapped and eaten before the bounty swings through the kitchen doors. The heat of the bag on your lap – your trusted lap – as Dad whizzes you home. Stomachs growl under the gathering smell of coconut peshwari or crispy Peking duck. You return, triumphant, to the glooming house, where tea lights have been lit, and plates are warming in the oven.

Steam drips at the kitchen windows and you're breathing a sweet Seville orange fug. The enormous cauldron is on the hob, and Mum is scrutinising a china saucer, tilting it steep, running her finger through the syrup and froth. The empty jars are baking in the oven. The big tin – full of paper parchment discs and doilies – is open on the table. It's marmalade day.

By the time the barbecue is sufficiently hot, the tide has risen up to meet the sinking sun. The four of you have retreated to a sloping rock beneath the cliffs. Somehow Dad has managed to bring the hot coals with him, and the old portable grill is now balanced perfectly level on its wonky green legs beside you.

The pork chops go on. They sizzle their mouth-watering steam into the late summer air. The crusty rolls are cut ready. The lid on the apple sauce is loosened. Crystal brine laps placidly at your conquered boulder. The flooded beach is all yours: quiet but for your happy chatter and the gentle sound of fat rendering to crisp-edged gold.

You can't remember a time when you didn't love pickled onions. Standing at the counter you fish one out with the plastic yellow pickled onion spoon. You hold it tight between finger and thumb and crunch it half away. You think of the mud shaken from the shallots, brought home from the allotment. Another crunch and you fish for another. Nanny at the kitchen table, tasked with peeling the brown skin from each little bulb. The green-white onions bobbing in a bowl of cold brine. The long, long wait. The repeated requests to open the first jar, until finally your wish is granted.

You crunch the other half of your second one, and then start another. No one else is around to tell you not to. You know you should eat some cheese and crackers with them, but then maybe *just one more*. The sharp, hot, sweet, sour crunch. How is it that raw onions and malt vinegar combine to make something so wonderful? You pay for this binge of the finite annual stock with a tummy ache. You regret nothing.

Evening meals under the old pergola. The enormous seagull watches you all from the roof. Bare feet and cooling air. Corn stuck between your teeth – extra butter on the naked cob, and more black pepper, rotating greedily for the last nibs of flavour. Just to make it last a little longer. Toast for pudding, grilled over the white coals, slavered in this year's runny strawberry jam. And then, with laughter, the jasmine flowers. Tiny white trumpets landed on the tablecloth, held to lips and sweet air sucked in through their nectar. A strange, delirious habit. A delicious discovery that no one can remember making, but which tastes like summer evenings.

First the juicy salsa, then the green guacamole, then the sour cream and chives. Salsa again, guacamole, then sour cream. Salsa, guacamole, sour cream. Repeat. Sweet-savoury dust coats your fingertips as you continue this perfect cycle through the Tex-Mex trio. No point licking them until the session is over – and with the house to yourself, who's to say you can't finish the lot? You'll let the dipping chain continue until you're wiping out the corners of the plastic tray, or until you hear the crumb-rattle of the empty Dorito bag.

You have the cookbooks out again and you're turning every single glossy page. Saliva gathers under your tongue, around your teeth. Your eyes devour the flavours of the photography on the right, scan the list of ingredients on the left. Your sheet of scrap paper from the cupboard is being torn into ever smaller squares, as you mark each recipe you want to make.

A thud travels through the floor and into the high heels of your shoes, quickly followed by another. With a roaring rustle, everyone sits down, and conversations erupt across the hall. Heavy gowns are shrugged off shoulders, red wine sloshed into glasses. Small saucers of yellow soup are sniffed and inspected as they slop along the line each side of the table. Noses wrinkle. Your stomach grumbles. Your knot of bread is already buttered, and you are ready to fill your stomach. Someone drops a coin into a glass nearby and cheap Shiraz is swallowed by its careless owner. You hear a pebble-plop across from you: a two-pence piece in someone's soup. The games have started swiftly.

Soup barely slurped and it's time for mains. This is the part that makes you nervous: the sharing. You are at the hands of other people's portion judgement, and you don't trust a soul. Especially not the group of boys to your right. Stainless steel dishes are brought and deposited at uneven intervals along the table: chicken breasts, sauce, mashed potatoes, steamed vegetables. Serving spoons are seized and you are poised, eagle-eyed, ready to object at the first hint of foul play. The potatoes nearest to your right are scraped clean when they reach you, but another tray arrives from the left, thanks to a group further down who tend to prioritise their bottles of wine from Tesco over the college menu. Then two chicken trays meet at your plate, and you take advantage of the extra mushroom sauce available to you as a result. It's every student for themselves, after all.

You see the windows are all fogged up as you approach the glow of the kitchen from the garden. You drag your suitcase through the door and suddenly it's hugs and wagging tail and coats off and *how was the journey*. You soak in the smell of cooking, the warmth of the room and the familiar clutter on every surface. Dad lines up the tumblers for gin and tonics and Mum fills a bowl with chilli flavoured crisps. You know she will be making a favourite. The salmon, she says. I know you like that one. With the bacon bits and the wilted lettuce. With those little crispy potatoes in the oven. You take a seat at the table. You beam. You are home.

The first time you cook for him, he hovers nervously by your side, trying not to show it. You bring a tote bag full of fresh ingredients to his shared kitchen and ask where the knives and chopping boards are. He doesn't usually chop things, he says. Buys green beans or asparagus, already portioned-up by nature. Together, you check the allergen labels of every packet. He washes the things you need, soaping them up carefully over the sink and passing you the utensils, still dripping.

You make vegetable chilli: colourful and thick with spice. You pile it onto a tray of tortilla chips, layer cheese, and bake it in their little oven till it bubbles. You dollop on soured cream and freshly mashed avocado, squeeze lime and scatter coriander leaves. You sit either side of the tray and talk and scoop and shovel.

You have a photo of his first bite, the amazement on his face, the glee beating from the girl behind the camera. You think it's easy, that it's just about curated ingredients, due diligence, gentle awareness. It is a number of months before you understand how many hurdles he must have quietly conquered while you made that meal for him. It is many more months before you realise how long this journey through food anxiety will take.

You have to admit the chips are some of the best in Barry. The restaurant might have mixed reviews, and you've seen what goes on behind the 'specials' menu, but every time you watch the chef toss those golden chips in a bowl of salt, and carry the generous mound to a table, you dream of malt vinegar steam and crispy edges. Most shifts you're on your feet through mealtimes, starved and snatching one or two of those crunchy bits from the bottom of the bowl when the kitchen porter isn't looking. You hate tipping untouched food into the slop of waste. Especially the chips.

You feel like the snot in your nose is going to freeze solid, but you're grinning from inside your furry hood. You've just stepped off the rink, but kids and adults are still hurtling around it – none of the short-paid time slots here. In winter, ice rinks are set up all over the city for anyone to use. You unclip the skates and hurry your woolly socks back into your cold boots. Then you walk slowly – strange how still and flat the ground feels under the soles of your feet – over to join the queue.

Your first Beaver Tail is hot between your mittens, steaming, cooling down rapidly. You eat it quickly and joyfully. The outside is crispy with cinnamon and sugar, coating your lips, warming you up from the inside. He takes a photo of you mid-bite, holding the paper bag right up to your face, clutching either side of the golden oval inside. You both laugh, knowing how gleefully you'll tell this one. Bear Paws.

Beaver Tails. Sugared gifts of conversation back in Wales.

You start walking as you eat, heading over to Parliament Hill, where the sun promises to set into a frozen spill of sherbet pinks and blues.

I know it means we're having pasta again but—

He interrupts to remind you, once more, that you both love pasta, so what's the problem? *Especially this one.* He grins, rubbing his hands together like a cartoon character.

So you start chopping. The aubergine into padded cubes, the two peppers into squares, the garlic cloves pressed under the wet blade's side, the courgette cut into long, thin quarters then down into even chunks. Lastly, the red onion: shelled from its stubborn skin, wedged and broken into petals – swiftly, before the tears spring further down your cheeks. All into the tray, some herbs from the cupboard, a twist of the pepper grinder and spoon of salt. You take the slippery olive oil bottle and swirl it upside down over the vegetables. Then you roast it all (high heat to stop it steaming itself to a wet slop) turning it all over once or twice with the wide wooden spatula. You boil the twists of pasta, extractor fan on full. The kitchen is smelling sweet and sharp. A last toss of the tray and you sneak in a splash of balsamic, a tiny drizzle of clear honey, to help those curling edges catch and caramelise. You decide to add some chilli flakes, and a few more fennel seeds. All fan favourites in this hungry house of two.

When it's time, you turn off the oven and tip the steaming pasta straight into the mix. You add more salt and pepper, some of the extra virgin olive oil from the cupboard, and finally the goat's cheese. Crumbing knobs nicked from the wrapper, stirred in to melt and meld, picking up every sticky bit of flavour in that tray. This, you think…this is more than the sum of its parts. *This is the best thing in my day.*

It's three days past the shortest night of the year. Your skin is pricked with goosebumps as you pile layers back onto your shivering body. The sea was like cold, liquid glass; sharp and deep and silky. With the sun gone but the sky still pale there were no reflections to obscure its surface, but pearl skin magnified under the water's clear lens. And below, the beach submerged.

Back on the shore you dress beside the smoking barbeque, pour cider into plastic cups and hum in the lilac light. It is almost 10 p.m. when you take your first bite, mingling the careful plait of ketchup and tangy mustard sauce, grinning while you chew. Your three best friends, sat between split rock on the shore of that hidden beach, grin, too. By the time you walk home through the deep grass and brambles, it is past 11 p.m. The flowers have filled the quiet air with scent and the stars are only just beginning to arrive.

You unlock the back door and go outside, colander in hand. The branches are flopping out into the doorway, and already you can see some scarlet baubles shining in the midday sun. You turn right and survey your green forest of tomato plants. Red and orange flashes under leaves, behind thick woody stalks. Already your mind is calmer. Already you are absorbed in the task of filling the colander with the latest crop of 'golden wonder' and 'little tom'.

You didn't used to understand why she did it, not once you were old enough to have better things to do. But all on their own accord, things seem to have come back around. You feel the greenhouse scent gathering on your fingers as you pick. You tut at the taut skin of numerous tomatoes, split at the stalk where they have been plucked. The weather is hot, and their grow bags are over-crowded – exactly as your mother said they would be. You smile because you know she is always right. When you've crouched and reached and tumbled all the swollen fruit into your pail, you straighten up, grab the watering can, and get to work.

When you make the gravy, you channel every time you made it under her tuition. When you make the gravy, everything else is just coming together. The meat is ready and resting under foil, the peas are simmering, the potatoes are getting their last crisping in the hot oven and the bread sauce is keeping warm on the hob.

You add the flour first; scrape it around, picking up all the oil and fat and colour in the roasting tin. Then, when a dark and gnarly paste is formed, you add the stock. It bubbles in the centre, a heated ring in the metal tray's base. You scrape and stir, blending it all into a viscous soup. Lots of seasoning. A spoonful of cranberry sauce. Then – and this is your own addition – a teaspoon of Marmite. Finally, a splash of wine from the middle of the table, and more stock to loosen it all up. Lift the meat on its board with the carving fork and, holding it steady, tip the whole thing up and carefully pour the juices into the pan.

Now everything is done. Now, taste it. Season it some more.

Then take the boat out of the cupboard (again, you forgot to warm the boat, she always warms it first) and pour all that gravy out, from the corner of the lifted tray, and into the gravy boat. It's ready, you say, proud, untying your apron at the back.

RHIWDDOLION VALLEY, ERYRI.

1.37 P.M.

You're sat on a small rock – one of the few not covered in thick, spongy moss – overlooking the velvet dip of this unknown Eden. Below you, the water cackles over boulders and fallen branches, in a gentle springtime flow.

Just across the stream is Tŷ Coch, smug and squat to the ancient hill, its doors and windows open in the sun.

A laugh arrives from further down the valley. A family member, carrying tin cans and heavy vegetables.

The sky is deep blue behind the lichened fingers of the trees. A breeze comes once in a while, slipping through your knitted sleeves. There is constant birdsong, and will be, right up until the stars come out.

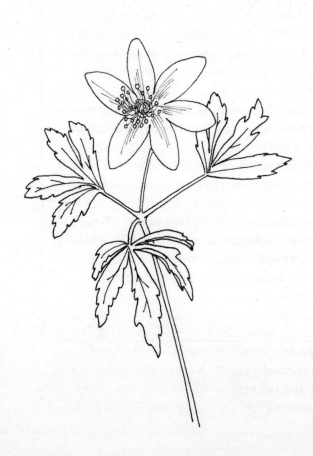

MOUNTAIN POOLS
AND NEOPRENE

The first swim doesn't happen until after sunset. The wind has settled down and the crags cradling the lake are shadowy and purple. We zip up the tent and creep to the crescent edge of Llyn Gwynant. A quick photo: bare-faced and grinning in our unplanned matching outfits. For a moment, we go laughing back to the playground of our primary school, and that same fur-hooded coat we both owned one winter.

The last light is pooling weakly in the lake's reflection. We step in and, emboldened by each other's presence, we wade through the long shallows, sucking air between our cheeks, cooing and hooting about the cold. Finally, thigh deep, I give up waiting for the shelf to slope off beneath my feet. I push my arms out in front of me, let go of the slippery lakebed and surge into the water. My lungs roar a sigh, emptying themselves of all the day's driving and hiking and crouching and talking. My pale skin glows just under the surface, dissolving into the twilight ink below. And that old familiar feeling returns. It settles into all the lines of my body, filling all the gaps.

Breathe in. Breathe out. Smile. Laugh. Let the muscles uncoil and relax into the weightless underwater space. You are here, swimming in this lake, this plane of shadow and mountain, sinking under dusk. You are here. You are here.

It is a few years since I finally returned to water, but conflict still tussles quietly around it. I admit to myself that different hesitations have followed me to the water's edge throughout my life, and now that 'wild swimming' has become something worthy of inverted commas, those hesitations can sometimes feel like failures. I often want to write about swimming, but there is a part of me, made shy by all the memoirs and Instagram accounts, which thinks I shouldn't. I'm not committed enough – I'm not a member of the tribe.

'I need to swim,' I said to Imogen on the phone. She knows north Wales better than I do. She worked there as a trainee doctor and is on first name terms with lots of the peaks and lakes. The map is dense with opportunities; a reliable bet for some wild water therapy. 'I need to gather some fresh moments,' I told her, 'for my writing.'

But I needed to swim because I've hardly had the chance to in this latest version of life. Because I wanted to remind myself how easy it can be: how simple to slip into a lake and call it yours. To escape. To scoop up the last September warmth with the help of my oldest friend.

So we designed this small adventure around bodies of water. We are here for the weekend, putting a few hills between ourselves and the quickening weeks of normal life. We are here to come back to each other for a few days; to talk, to breathe, to swim.

The last light leaves, and we shrug on heavy dry robes. Mine, borrowed, drowns my limbs in padded microfleece. It is the first time I have ever used one, and I marvel at the stillness of my muscles, so used to shivering their way into hasty layers. I think of the women I have seen wearing these as coats down cobbled high streets: the price-tagged cloak of honour.

We strap on our sandals and squelch straight to the campsite's shower block. Steam can be seen rising from the cubicles and into the chilly night. Pyjama-clad pairs come and go with their toiletry bags, settling in before an early start. Behind us, headlights roll over gravel as those who left the city after work finally arrive, to pitch tents beneath invisible giants. I think how sweet their morning discovery will be; how they will open canvas under dewy mountain shade and tumble into the sharp majesty of Eryri.

Our own morning is spent slowly, hammocked in our folding chairs. Nearby, rings of men in thin shorts and expensive soft-shell jackets compare gear and local knowledge. Wet grass and water on the boil. Group excursions to the sinks to wash up last night's dishes. Metal camping mugs are emptied, water bottles filled, and long days' journeys cheerfully begun.

The shallow river slipping by behind the hawthorns is silent. We sip our coffee under their short branches, and let the sun climb high before readying our own things to head out.

We traverse the long edge of Llyn Gwynant and then we're out of the trees and gaining height. The air is thicker than we thought it would be. None of the promised wind, but pillowy clouds and a persistent sun. By the time we approach the foot of the valley, our layers are all folded into our backpacks and the deep jade pools of the Watkins waterfalls beckon more than ever. Gushing mountain water spilling out from one and into another. A chain of rippling jewels draped in the lap of Yr Wyddfa.

There is something very freeing about dedicating the trip specifically to swimming. Usually, stripping off to swim is a by-product of already being in some special place. It is a do-we-don't-we dance between staying dry and taking the plunge. Under-preparing and over-thinking, a battle of bravery and convenience. This approach, however, with the Watkins pools at the heart of our day's agenda, clears all that clutter out of the way.

We climb further up the valley, past the first pools that are already taken. We go on past two more plunges which, though not yet occupied, are exposed to the curiosity of walkers on the main path above. I don't fancy stopping to undress in what feels like an amphitheatre. So we carry on, holding out for something better further up.

This is the first time I have ventured up the Watkins path for the sole purpose of enjoying the pools, but I am surprised to see so many others doing the same. On previous climbs to the summit, I have hiked past these pools and been mesmerised by the sight of the pebbles, quivering and bluish on the riverbed. The icy baths, scoured out by the ancient rush of mountain rain, weren't a good idea in early April, when hands were fisted tight in gloves and snow still patched the peaks. But the seduction of the pools has led me back here in the mild breath of September, and the selfish part of me is disappointed to now be sharing them with crowds of strangers.

We cross the river just below the sluice gate, hopping boldly over stones that rock against the currents. We venture on, using the main path now, because Imogen can remember seeing a photo taken from an 'infinity' pool further up towards the slate quarry. I'm happy to extend the search, to defer the decision that needs to be made. It's a sunny, busy Saturday on the side of Yr Wyddfa. All those other water tourists got here first and I'm worried that whatever we settle with, is not going to match the wild tranquillity I had planned in my mind.

I have a fraught relationship with the growing PR around outdoor swimming. It seems to splinter me into different parts. One part wishes that my old private places, my favourite coves in Pembrokeshire (which of course aren't mine at all) could remain empty and quiet. Another part I don't admit, is the one that feels jealousy; resentment towards all the people who are better at it than me, who get out and into the water more, who brave all the months I never would. The ones who actually call themselves 'wild swimmers'.

But I also appreciate the paths these swimmers are forging, the normalcy they are creating around that unexplainable urge to get closer, to get in and under the surface. I often feel afraid to swim in places I have never seen another person swim. I like to seek out spots that I know are tried and tested, where swimmers are no surprise for the daily dog walkers. Though of course I want them to be entirely deserted when I get there.

The recent surge in outdoor dipping has seen territory open up all over the place. Imogen tells me that gangs of women now meet for the high tide on Penarth seafront – every morning, with their brightly coloured floats. This coastline of our childhood, spent skimming stones and squelching in tidal mud, was rarely ventured into back then.

Groups campaign for more access to safe reservoirs, for the opening up of public waterways, for cleaner rivers and for the right to enjoy the simple act of getting into them. Cold-water fanatics have always been there, but now it seems they're being noticed, and in this busy world of noise and arguments, more are joining their ranks. Climbing into a body of water under open sky is now a section on the bookshelves; no longer just a simple giving in to bodily instinct.

All this popularity has brought another type of nervousness. Instead of being the only one who wants to swim, now I often feel like I'm the only one who isn't truly dedicated. I feel like the 'wild swimmers', armoured by bravery and dryrobes, are in a club, and that I don't meet the criteria for entry. I see photos of women, grinning at the frosty edges of a reservoir, and I think how easy it all looks; how the problem must be me.

Back when Andrew and I were living in Huddersfield, and the country was entering another winter lockdown, I had a desperate urge to have one more swim. It was the first day of November, blustery and overcast, but I had a plan, and I was determined. We drove to Todmorden and then up one of its steep sides, parking at the bottom of a footpath which led to the 'highest beach in the UK': a small sliver of freshwater sand cornering an industrial reservoir. The pictures online had shown a crystal shore, busy with families; children splashing and laughing and generally not giving any clues that this 'beach' lay eighty feet above sea level and sixty miles inland.

On the ascent to Gaddings Dam, my conviction wavered. We were both wrapped in winter layers; my head under a soft knitted hat, my hands tucked under my elbows. There was no one else to be seen on the footpath, and I scanned the mulchy puddles nervously for signs of ice.

When we reached the moorland summit, my resolve almost dissolved in the wind. Grey water slapped at the grey sky. A group of walkers in black puffer jackets hurried, heads down, along the reservoir wall. We walked the long way around and reached the deserted beach. I, determined for this not to be one of those failed missions, pulled my feet out of my boots and began passing clothes to Andrew. I hesitated before keeping my woolly hat on, the way I'd seen the Blue Tits (a growing network of outdoor swimmers) do it, Instagramming from their giddy meetups. I jogged into the wind with as much conviction as I could muster.

The cold had never hurt like that before, and I laughed like a maniac. The numbness I thought I could rely on never arrived, only needling pain in my feet and toes. I retreated, but then, already splashed, I rushed back in. Only a few seconds later, but satisfied that my shoulders had dipped below the wind-scraped waves, I snatched my micro towel from Andrew and dressed as quickly as I could. I had to take my hat off because it was cold and sodden at the back.

My jaw was chattering and slow to shape its words, and my feet ached. I tried to stomp those needles out of them with every step back down the hill, pleased that I had dared to carry on, but wondering why on earth had I felt compelled to do so.

Early this year, Imogen and her partner started swimming in a hillside pond near their house in Cwmbran – almost every week. I am in open admiration of this; not only for the temperature in wintertime, but for the time they manage to carve out to do it.

We leave the main path again and tussock-hop over boggy grass. I reassure myself that, with my neoprene shoes, I will be fine. I was always the first of us to go running down the beach, the first to say: *don't hesitate, you'll only make it harder!* But I also don't like being cold, and I'm learning that it's not always just about a state of mind, or a matter of will. Sometimes the water is just flipping freezing.

We scramble over an old rubble wall and up onto an

outcrop to see if we can survey the water from above. We're following a tributary now, and can see a shallow, rippling curve before its path disappears beyond the long grass and out of sight. Below us, the river bend: the open cut of root-woven earth.

We decide to give up and follow the rivulet back to the path to make our way down to join the rest of the swimmers in the gorge below. But only a few minutes along its edge, we see a rock face that, once over the bank of reeds, turns out to be cradling a hidden pool. Water tumbles into one end and is held among the rocks by a thick log at the other. A natural infinity pool.

There is hesitation, still. There is no obvious place to leave our bags, and the water looks cold under the granite's shade; less welcoming than the sun-splashed emeralds we had seen earlier. But we are entirely alone. There are no paths nearby; no sign, even, that this place is here. I climb down onto a tufted ledge beside the water and spot a yellow banana skin. This is a swimming place. It is pre-approved.

The decision is made, and balanced on each of our chosen perches, we change into our swimsuits. I put on my old water shoes and step onto the rocks. The pool is beautiful from down here, tucked into the mountain and fed generously with its water. I go in, carefully over the loose boulders, up to my knees. Then, emptying my mind, leaving no space for second thoughts, I surge forwards and into the deep. It is a glorious kind of cold, a thrilling one: a smile wider than the valley and deeper than the hill.

Sometimes, for all the nervousness and uncertainty, the missed opportunities, the forced enjoyment…sometimes, going in can feel like the best decision you've ever made. It's like feeling everything and nothing simultaneously. It's so straightforward. Closer to yourself and further from your life than anywhere else. Closer to the landscape – as close as possible. If I was asked to define the word 'bliss',

I think this secret pool – the way it holds my body in its clarity – would be my answer.

We take turns swimming towards the fall, floating, submitting, letting the current carry us back towards the shallow rocks. I stay until I know I should get out, until the numb creeps seductively to my core. Then, shoulders still under the water, we slip our swimming costumes off. I feel the cold silk of the river on every surface of my skin. It's only the second time in my life that I've known this liberation, and I think of the brave woman on my Instagram feed who does it all the time. It's a fleeting freedom, unhindered except for the wary knowledge that the sun is high and hikers swarm the hills nearby.

We leave the pool and hurry into our warm layers. A stream of half-sensical elation chatters out of us, and we eat two mini pork pies from my rucksack, a toast to our success.

In *The Living Mountain*, Nan Shepherd wrote: 'I have walked myself with brilliant young people whose talk, entertaining, witty and incessant, yet left me weary and dispirited, because the hill did not speak.' As we begin our descent, I wonder if I might have felt the experience more deeply if I had been alone...if the mountain water would have whispered to me more intimately, in the way the lochs spoke to Nan. But the thought dissolves immediately with the knowledge that without Imogen, I wouldn't be here at all. Going out to swim in unconventional places is not as easy as many of my favourite books would make it seem, especially for a lone young woman. Most of my boldest adventures have, for the better, been embarked upon with a partner.

After a long wintering in Huddersfield, spent mostly indoors or up on the nearby moors, the weather warmed, and I began to search for somewhere closer to swim. I tried the local leisure centre, but it was too soon. Changing in draughty cubicles, mask still on, rushing to make the most of my time slot...only to enter an over-booked pool and swim close behind spluttering strangers. It felt uneasy. And the radio was so loud that I could hear its tinny music underwater.

As the weather warmed, I thought of looking for a group of swimmers I could join as a way to access new places, and, after such an isolated time, new people. There was no formal club in West Yorkshire, but there was a Facebook group which, once admitted into, could be used to find out where and when others were swimming nearby. After a few weeks of wallflower-watching, I finally dipped my toe in and responded to a post.

Four days later, I was driving into the low evening sun out of an old industrial pocket of town and into unexpected fields. I had detailed directions from someone kind who I had never met. I parked up, as instructed, behind a few other cars at the dead end of a lane. A few women had gathered beside a barrier at the mouth of a grassy track. The sign displayed was Yorkshire Water telling us not to swim. I looked around – and saw no evidence of the water it was referring to.

A few minutes and a short walk later, we were at the edge of a small and picturesque reservoir. The stone wall we had climbed was low and unwired, and a thin but well-worn path ribboned away from the notch we had utilised – not far from another sign that said, 'private property'. This was clearly a popular spot.

The water was smooth pink and green, a rectangle pooled into the grassy hills, stretched out under the lazy evening sky. When I entered it, I relaxed – the familiar feel of fresh water between my fingers washed away all the nervousness, the small talk, the battle I had fought to get here and not stay comfortably at home. In the water, I was among friends, and not much mattered except the way the dissolving sun danced on the ripples we had made. I couldn't recount a single one of those women's names, but they gave me that place with such simple generosity.

A few swam off to lap the perimeter, but I stayed near the bank, feeling surprisingly little pressure to go a stroke out of my comfort zone. I was encouraged to speak up if I felt cold, though the reservoir was quite welcome on my skin that evening. Still, I was pleased to find a range of approaches to the water. Wetsuits were readily accepted, and thick towels and hot tea waited for the quick change on the flattened grass afterwards. One woman, who had eased herself in very gently, then donned an ingenious home-made robe: two thick bath towels sewn together to make a poncho.

I had my new microfibre 'toncho' – a birthday gift from my mum which could roll into the smallest of bags, and which she sent along with a glossy wild swimming guide, full of photos that served as excellent day-dream fodder.

Swimming outside means undressing in public and leaving your belongings on the banks unattended. It means exposing your body to the elements and often, on our small and busy island, the gaze of passersby. It is, by definition, vulnerability. It's inevitable, then, that most men have historically not attached the same anxieties to swimming outside as I do.

To enter the water together is often the answer. It is safety in numbers: especially for those who might be nervous about the many restrictions on river and water access in the UK (I am not a natural rule breaker, I admit), or are inexperienced when it comes to choosing a suitable spot. But this is a shame, because for many newcomers, group settings can be just as intimidating as solitude. It also puts a bit of an official stamp on the activity, making it seem much more 'all or nothing' than something as simple as climbing into water should.

When Imogen and I arrive back at the campsite, we have already decided: before our muscles can relax too long, we've put on our squelching water shoes and are pumping up the paddle board. The site is quiet, most of its occupants now making their descent from Yr Wyddfa's summit. As the afternoon shadows begin to stretch, we drop the board into the silent river and – slipping behind the hawthorns – float out together onto an almost empty lake.

Llyn Gwynant is sparkling this time. Imogen stirs the surface of the lake, paddling us slowly across the top of its unknown. I sit cross-legged at her feet, letting my fingertips drag through the water's silk. Neither of us speak. We're listening to the gentle repetition of ripples around smooth plastic strokes. We've got our eyes fixed on the same sacred spot – we're heading for Clogwyn y Fulfran, known to climbers as Elephant Rock.

In the middle of the lake, we swap places. The manoeuvre is clumsy and comical, full of unspoken fear of the inky depths camouflaged by the shimmer.

As we near our destination, Imogen recalls how she swam from the roadside of the lake all the way across to the crag with a keen group of wet-suited medics, fluorescent floats in tow. I look back over my shoulder. There is a glint in the distance, a sequin moving along the far edge of Llyn Gwynant – a car on the road heading towards the Watkins carpark.

Clogwyn y Fulfran resembles a memory collected a long time ago, somewhere in British Columbia. Its hard granite disappears, straight down, into the lake: a cliff face among pointed pines. We push the board onto a ledge sloping just under the water's surface, tuck the paddle into the elastic straps, and then climb up onto the first level. The rock face has a few shelves, which can be easily reached by those wanting to jump, and another, much higher, which is more difficult to access.

We jump from the lowest level, gleefully, being caught almost immediately by the lake. As I climb back onto the ledge, I look down at the glassy water, its depth revealed in the shadow of the rock. I think of this jumping platform as it really is: a cliff, hulking and ancient, cushioned right up to its chin by slinky rainwater.

We agree to let ourselves off the hook – to not try for the highest jump today. Neither of us is in the mood to push ourselves or prove anything impressive. Instead, igniting my childish self, I dive from the lower shelf over and again, thinking how rare it is to find the right conditions for a headfirst entrance. I gather threads of muscle memory, trying each time to make as little splash as possible, to point my toes, to spring from my feet and arc my body like a javelin.

In Huddersfield, I only joined that secret reservoir group for a handful of Sundays before we made our sudden decision to leave the UK and stay with Andrew's family for the summer. In Ontario, of course, I was spoilt for swimming choice. Despite living in the city, his parents' house is a ten-minute drive from the wide river, where you can park up among the trees and swim from a sandy life-guarded beach. As soon as I discovered this, we went as often as we could, staying in the placid water for as long as we liked, playing games, not wanting to return to the adult shore.

But it wasn't until our trip to Algonquin Park that I remembered just how free wild swimming is in Canada – and how deeply I knew this already. On the recommendation of our B&B host, we found ourselves wading into the mirrored reflection of the sunset just a few hours after arriving, entirely alone, the dark water like a warm blanket in the cool night air.

The next day, while cycling borrowed bikes along the old railway line, I stopped, stunned for a moment, at a gap in the trees. Looking out across the water, bordered with mossy rocks and evergreen islands, I realised that this is the world I had preserved in my mind: the Canada I had visited as a child and archived as a playground of perfect swimming. It is this which drew me so keenly to the base of Elephant Rock in north Wales. It is this which, at such a young age, taught me to love deeply the press of a lake on my bare skin.

In the UK, there are lots of rules in place to tell us where not to swim. Growing up by the sea, I always felt more confident there, knowing it didn't belong to anyone in particular, and that to swim from a beach was a generally acceptable thing to do. But beaches are often broad and exposed, the tides can be uncertain or, as in my mind, the pinch of a claw or sting of a jellyfish always a possibility. I still feel nervous whenever I enter the waves barefoot, much preferring the protection of my floppy neoprene shoes from Sports Direct.

Lakes, rivers and reservoirs hold their own special tranquillity, and I harbour a deep jealousy for those who live in places like Ontario, with long warm summers and every lake at their disposal.

We have already agreed the next morning to go back out on the lake. We're in no doubt that having Llyn Gwynant just outside the door of our tent provides an opportunity that really shouldn't be missed. Once the sun has crested the ridge above, we heave on our wetsuits and lower the paddle board back into the river. The stillness of the water is intoxicating. Out on the lake, beyond the ribbony weeds of the shallow plateau, we make our way towards the day's warmth. We can see it up ahead, lifting wisps of morning mist up from the surface of the lake, igniting it like smoke in the gentle sunlight.

It is a quiet and simple expedition. After twenty minutes, we turn back, knowing there is lots to do – we haven't even brushed our teeth yet. When we reach the mouth of the river,

I slip into the water, keen on the idea of swimming the last way back to our tent. The water is cold, and I feel heavy moving through it. I have Roger Deakin in my mind, with his journeys through the waterways of Britain, his casual frog's-eye voyages. His landmark book, *Waterlog*, has for years been inspirational to me. But I'm beginning to see that I would often use those pages as evidence of my own shortcomings. He made it look so easy, this regular immersion into unknown waters, his intimacy with the creatures who live there. But Roger Deakin and I are different. We are not diving from the same level jetty.

I grow tired before reaching the bank beside our pitch. I stand up and wade along the shallow edge, needing a break from the cold, and from the flies skitting around the water's surface.

We pack everything up just in time for the rainclouds to arrive, then drive up out of the valley and towards our final appointment. I've swum in Llyn Padarn before with Imogen, but this time we're entering it from a different side; just beside a bridge and a small string of cottages, and very close to the carpark of a favourite local café. We meet a band of her friends in this carpark, and head down to the water together. The sky is low and grey, and the wind is picking up some energy. The morning's languid float among sunlit mist could so easily have been a dream.

I feel nervous among these people who, I know, swim often in the open waters of north Wales. They are all laughing and at home, having used this corner of the lake many times before. But I know that this place belongs to everyone – to me as well – and I have spent the weekend reminding myself as much.

Perhaps it's the preparation of the last two days, or perhaps it's proof that my self-criticism is unfounded, but I'm the first out and into the deeper water. I swim quietly and cheerfully, soaking in this final treat before it's time to dry off and return to the city.

I know that this will be the last swim of the year for me. Once back in York I'll be busy with the run up to the book festival at work, with writing, with the hibernation instinct that comes with the cold weather. I know the reasoning – how alive cold-water swimming makes you feel – but for now, I'm a fair-weather dipper. I'll do lanes in the local leisure centre I'm sure and walk out in the bitter mornings when the frost is crunchy underfoot...but I won't be found in any lakes until next year.

I walk out of Llyn Padarn before I get too cold. First in, first out. I change slowly under the branches of a tree and notice raindrops beginning to land on the driftwood log in front of me. Soon, the others trickle out, each changing with well-practised efficiency. The wind is bringing more raindrops with it now, and we gather our things to go back up to the café for hot tea and spicy stew.

I spend too much time worrying that the frequency of my own swimming experiences do not match the level of joy I take from them. I interpret my failure to pursue this love of mine as cowardice or lack of dedication. But fear plays all sorts of roles in this story, and I'm realising that, actually, lots of the pages were not written by me.

I'm not a regular 'wild swimmer'. I think that one day if I find myself living by the sea again, or on a lake, I might be. But for now, I'm not. I swim in brief bursts, when the time and place is right, and I love it when I do.

Whether it's a one-time charge into the sea with friends, or a quiet bathe under all the colours of the evening sky, outdoor swimming can belong to anybody. Those moments, however they occur, are ours to keep for as long as we like. I think that even one perfect swim, if you take good care of it, is enough to last a very long time.

PORTHKERRY, SOUTH WALES.

2.45 P.M.

The old monks' path is sunk deep into the soil, a gloomy tunnel where dusk is already lurking. The banks are steep on either side, ancient hedgerows built up around the roots of their overgrown founders. The trees all meet overhead, some wrapped in knotted ivy ropes, some rubbing branches, creaking in the wind.

Another gust gathers noise in the wood and comes grumbling overhead, whirling any last leaves out into the field.

The tunnel is sheltered, frilled each side with glossy fern and bedded all the way down with soggy cornflakes – the bright confetti of beech trees, collected through autumn and cradled in this sheltered passageway.

The path leads you down from the lime washed church on the hill. Down, under the rainclouds and the salt-flecked gale, towards the old priory – a place now hidden, electric-gated, its boundaries trimmed neat in a dense variety of yew.

BETWEEN LINES

Slowly, the mornings are getting lighter. Each time I walk the river path, the mist on the water has lifted a little higher. Soon, the sunrise will be perfectly aligned with the train timetable, and I will be able to bathe in the cold, pink light while I wait on the platform edge.

For now, orange lights still glow as I reach the heavy arches of the station. Gloves still wrap my fingers and people walk at the pace demanded by an early Monday chill. The coffee I made at home has gone tepid in my hand. I reach my platform just in time, drop into a forward-facing window seat, and shed some layers.

Welcome on board this TransPennine Express service to Newcastle.

I watch the first light of the day ignite bellies of the lowest clouds, just as York slides south and the fields gather speed in the window. My book stays cold and uncreased in my bag. A hare sits bolt upright in the frost.

I am satisfied, content with observing the fast-creeping dawn, and the destination I'm in the process of reaching.

My thoughts, then, are free to go. Free to stay and sit at a soft simmer, or to slip down under the gentle distraction of the farmland I'm starting to know by sight.

The train takes me from one place name to another. In the trough of winter, I hardly even see the shape of the land that leads me there, with inky window reflections rendering much of the commute a slow teleport to where I need to be. I know the stops – *calling at Northallerton, Darlington, Durham, Chester-le-Street* – but learn nothing of the unlabelled spaces in between. They are a slideshow to sip coffee to; paintings hardly inhabited by other creatures, save the occasional welly-booted dog walker, or gawping pheasant. They are places as fictional to me as scenes in a film, observed always from the fixed angle of the train track, but never actually filling my nostrils, or being felt beneath my feet.

January rolls on and into February. Silvery fields fill with chocolate water. The river rises up, out of its tidy channel, lifting the tethered boats above their moorings. The riverside path disappears; along with the knuckles of the trees, the peeping bulbs, the trodden mulch of last year's leaves.

Our first spring in the city is prefaced with a flood; and with newly arrived neighbours who quickly become much-needed friends. I start, finally, to feel as though I have arrived in a place that is home. My sense of portability – of being somewhere in between – begins to fade.

The day the waters rise their highest, I walk down to the bottom of our street almost every hour. The pavement there breaks into steps which overlook the Millennium Walk. I count each step the Ouse has climbed, creeping itself right up to the first terrace's flowerpots.

The sky swells to children's picture book colours – peach and lilac and blue. Water, wide and fast, moves quietly past the end of the road. It sweeps its twigs and branches with it, leaves spinning in spontaneous eddies. Everything else around the river's course is remarkably still. Everything is under water, standing submerged in the steady one-way flow. A ceaseless slipping by in one direction.

The day dissolves into street-lit night. The pigeons are settled in their trees, hunched and muttering, no doubt confused by their new proximity to the water. It has risen right up to where the chestnut tree forks. It has risen to the neck of an old streetlamp that stands calmly bolted to the newly claimed riverbed. And though its wires are deep under the current, the lantern's familiar light spills out over the water: folds and ripples, milky brown and hurrying, impatient swirls unsure of where to wrap themselves. You can see the surface catch on hidden obstacles below: the bench, the railings, the information board.

The greylags have stopped their moaning. All is quiet, except the rushing of the spill. The lamp lights the night just as it always does.

We find out that this is not unusual behaviour for our river: a regular cycle of muddied paths and jet washing. Nothing for us at number 18 to be concerned about. And hasn't York always been here? Here, on this floodplain where two fickle rivers meet.

Lichened slate roofs. Home-time traffic. Skeletal branches lace the skyline. A red sun, cut sharp as a disc of shell, sinks swiftly into its lilac haze. Flight trails, still lit, seam the sky, which has swallowed its ruby and is ready for sleep.

In March we scoop up from the tarmac and look down at the shrinking star of Heathrow's runways. There is a patchwork quilt laid out below me. Each square is claimed by someone. Each hedge-frilled road is numbered. I am looking at a catalogue of ownership; boundaries which have been marked, fenced, named and haggled since long before the roads were paved.

The map soon becomes a myriad of pixels, clustering smaller into the dense nuclei of towns and tiny cities. In a matter of hours, we will be hovering over a different patchwork quilt, landing on much colder tarmac, and we will be seamlessly transferred from the temperate aeroplane's climate into the heated concourse of Toronto airport. The city's winter air need never touch my skin before I am teleported to another city where, at last, my body can begin to understand that it is somewhere new. The light is brighter than it should be now. The wind is sharper.

I think about how much I like to be able to walk from one destination to the next. To understand my surroundings as a web of physical changes, rather than disconnected dots on an imaginary diagram.

There is a hot air balloon in the sky. We find our neighbours on the pavement outside both our houses. They are showing their little girl and pointing. Our adult delight fills the quiet street, and we each imagine what it would be like to be the ones up there, looking down. The balloon shows just how wide and deep the ocean of sky above us is. It is small and far away, and yet not very high at all. Its crisp lines and perfect detail remind us that yes, it is real, it is really there. Water simmers in a pan on the hob. Another tear-drop balloon rises from behind the rooftops.

The split and splintered trees – casualties from this year's storms – are mostly gone by spring. Their hanging grey husks spirited away, chopped into neat piles for seasoning.

At Darlington, I notice a fern growing inside the station's wall. It has enough light from the grimy crescent windows, and enough water from the green slime drips, to succeed. Bursts of smaller plants star the brickwork around it, a constellation of colour in the gloom. My two favourite things about Darlington train station are the cookie cutter shapes punched out of the metal girding that holds the roof, and the lemon juicer points carved into the stone where each of those sweeping archways meet.

By now, the mornings are bright and damp. We crawl out of the industrial cavern and continue north. New branches are waxy and red with buds. Rabbits' tails flash in the grass. My toes feel warm in my boots.

I fall back into the chapter in my hands and miss the familiar landmarks of Durham. In the first months of this new commute, I would have made sure each time I boarded that I was on the right-hand side where, forty minutes into the journey, I would see the bailey arrive in my window, cushioned with trees and crowned in golden brick. Often, I sit on the other side now. Often this place of mixed and pungent memories slips by, unseen, between two turns of a page.

We find the occasional pocket of time to venture out at weekends. We do the research, ask around for recommendations, and then we punch a postcode into Google Maps and let our satnav take us from York to somewhere new. I try to ingest the shape of the journey, to keep track of the inclines and open straights, to understand the spaces in between. But they are flickering fields behind high hedgerows. They are names on signposts pointing elsewhere. They are anonymous towns filled with other lives, only hinted at from the dual carriageway.

I find, as I have in other new homes, that I feel isolated by the unknown geography around me. I know my street, my little stretch of river. I know the rooftops from my attic study and the way the light rises and falls over their tiles. But I have no context to my location. Getting out of the city feels like a much bigger job than it should, because it is all unknown. Where do I start? Where do I begin to colour in the empty picture – sketched by online reviews and 'Top Ten Walks Near York' – with the press of my own boots?

Most weeks I continue to deepen the lines I've already made: from home to the railway station, from home to the shops, from home down to the river and out into the nearby fields, and back again.

Quite suddenly, there is the annual explosion of rapeseed flower. It takes about a week to happen. I track the yellow from my train window, brighter every morning, spreading like a disease from the sunny centre of each field to its shady edges.

I peel layers from my usual outfits and swap my boots for plimsolls. As my train crosses the bridge over the Tyne, its water below is often bristling with sunlight. But the air when the doors shudder open still makes me cross my arms. The wind snaking through the streets that take me to my office finds its way between buttons and inside collars.

I sit with my neighbour in her garden, knees close and cardigan-wrapped. The sun is still awake and it's almost dinner time. I finish my mug of tea as she tells me about the friends she has made in the last few months of nursery home-times. Purple campanula creeps along the wall behind her.

One afternoon, when I am working from home, a map is pushed through our letterbox. It marks all the independent businesses in York, dotting them along the colourful lines of the city centre. I fold away the lists and adverts and stick this square of land to the kitchen cupboard. I examine it while the glass plate in the microwave revolves. I memorise the shapes and names beyond our little house.

There is a field, not far north of York, less than ten minutes into my train journey, which has become a crimson sea of blooming poppies. I wonder why they chose this field, this square napkin of scarlet among the vast quilt of Yorkshire's green.

I start to catch the early train more often. Sometimes I take the bike along the river path and lock it up near the bridge before finishing my journey to the station on foot. I fast forward the beginning of my day. I push the pedals hard through the high gears, rushing against wind, past all the usual walkers. I slow down and weave between our stubborn colony of geese, now established for their summer residence and never willing to stir for my two tyres.

One morning my new skirt comes untucked and catches between the back brake and the wheel. I go into work with a smear of black bicycle grease among folds of poppy-red cotton.

Another morning, as I'm spinning the digits on my bike lock, a pigeon rouses itself in the oak tree overhead and drops its first business of the day on my jeans.

Sometimes I leave the bike at home so that when my train comes in that evening, I can turn right from the station, climb the city wall and let it lead me half the way home. From up there, I can watch the late evening sink behind the rooftops, dissolving the long day into a tangerine glow between each notch in the old stone ramparts. Sometimes there are hot air balloons hanging in the haze, too.

In August, I land on the other side of the Atlantic again. Whenever we are in Canada, we drive everywhere. We climb into the car in one part of the city, and out of it in another. We fly along highways which cut straight lines through endless forest.

'Wilderness' is something beyond the treeline. But it is there – and I am reminded how much we rely on way-marked routes. How we are always following the tracks of others, safely enjoying the world from our established footpaths. Even 'wilderness', when we do venture in, has been marked by someone on a map and threaded with at least a few dotted lines.

From the passenger seat, I realise that all the journeys I make are along ready-made lines. Even when faced with an open field in Scotland, unused to my right to roam, I seek out sheep tracks and desire lines that I can follow.

I consider how young children run in all directions, not yet orienteering themselves unconsciously in relation to existing lines. I remember jumping down from the boardwalks in Cosmeston Park, squashing our own routes through the reeds. I think of how often I have walked my favourite lane coming down from St Twynnells, tunnelled, winding and damp. Its steep banks, frilled with glossy ferns, hide the shape of the land around, and all the open views beyond. I recall the times I have followed my father over the unmarked cliffs and rocks at St Govan's Head, thinking as I tread behind how deeply he knows this place. Not its paths, but its edges, caves and contours.

Six cygnets, bigger than their mother, stream through the stagnant green above the lock. I am racing the rainclouds home. The wind blows. A rumble. I push the handlebars up and onto our street, wheels turning in the metal grooves fixed to the steps. The first fat drops spot the tarmac.

Sunflower heads become hunched in their dry fields.

I take the early train for the first time in weeks. I dress in the gloom and assume it will be light by the time I leave – but then it's time, and I'm fumbling in the alley, trying to find the lights I strapped onto my bike last year.

The first fallen leaves are curled like onion skins along the pavements.

Even as the train pulls away, the light is still struggling to rise much higher than the treeline. The small pockets of mist in certain fields are like wadding – woolly pools filling the dimples in the land. I make the most of what I can see: the horizon, the folds we're speeding through. I look far out across the hills and remind myself that these are the contours of a map laid out in front of me. The *real* land, so often translated into lines. I imagine their ripples as seen from the sky, picture the nearby towns and cities tucked into their glacier-carved cradles. A continuous sweep of shapes, all gilded by the same diluted sun.

I hurry out of the office a few minutes later than preferred. I reach the junction just as the lights have turned red again, and shift on impatient feet while the cars and lorries swing around the wide bend. Leaves and empty crisp packets are whipped up in fast spirals.

I follow my well-trodden track through the centre of Newcastle, weaving around all the early evening activity on the pedestrian shopping street, the different age groups gathered around Grey's Monument, the varying paces on the road leading down, straight down, to the great heavy archways of the railway station. I pass a busy bus stop. Wind sweeps around the junction corner up ahead. Pink sparks skitter across the paving stones. A stub rolls under hurried feet. Jewellery glints behind washed and polished glass. Pigeons hobble in and out of bus lanes.

Ten minutes later, I am settled on a warm carpeted seat in my usual carriage, and the city is breaking up into its suburbs. I listen to a young couple at the nearby table seat, arguing over an apartment that they *can* and *can't* afford to rent.

The train travels between rock and earth, along deep grooves blasted by Victorian men.

Another ten minutes; out past Durham and into the countryside, beyond its terraced edges. I decide the evening is much darker than it should be. Gloomy and moody and glum. Outside, the glowing bodies of seagulls rise up from freshly tilled, chestnut-brown fields.

Within a week, I think, my commute will go back to the flash of orange streetlamps and my own reflection.

We leave the hot aerosol climate of the gym. It is a clear night, and stars stud the velvet sky, but we have been told to hurry because clouds are on their way. We park up on a gravelled patch behind the university sports centre and lock the car. We find our way down the dark path between the trees, past the model Mercury, then Venus, heading for the silhouetted cap of the observatory. Our neighbour meets us in the red light, and we climb the metal skeleton inside.

The roof is on rollers, a loose helmet to be swivelled by hand. Our neighbour reaches up and the rectangle of sparkling sky rotates above us. Coordinates are tapped into a whirring laptop. The telescope hums as it turns to find its target.

First, it's Jupiter: a streaky golden globe. Another planet, right there, round and real. Not a photo or a reproduction, but a planet.

And then the moon, like cracked porcelain, blaring with white light. Lines track its surface, crossing fine rings and pockmarks. Lines I've never seen before. I gasp at the sight of our most familiar nightly landmark, shining huge in my wide eye. The lower edge, cast in a sliver of shade, shows the hard shapes of craters as they curve away from us.

Us, three friends huddled together in this tiny dome on a Tuesday night, urgently searching for planets and moons which have always been there.

Autumn hesitates and the first frost is shy to come. Each day that I work from home, I put on my boots and coat before it's time to sit at the keyboard, and step outside. I go down to the river to see how it's doing. I observe the different light on different mornings. I walk as far up towards the fields as I have time for (though sometimes a little further) and then go back again.

One rainy morning on my way back along the path I spot my neighbours up ahead: one, in her yellow raincoat and welly-boots, being carried by the other.

'How come you're out in this?' my neighbour asks. I tell him that I like to go outside before I sit down at my desk, that I create a little commute for myself. 'You're mad,' he tells me, holding out a palm to the rain. But I explain that the more weather, the better.

I've been asked to organise an event in York. I leave the house in a rush at 5 p.m., take Millennium Walk without thought, and meet a thick layer of slime, deposited by the most recent overflow. At the venue, I see an old print of the river, flanked by sloping, silty banks. I realise that the concrete lines, which now hem the Ouse and the Foss, are the reason I can be so close to them every morning.

After the authors have done their readings, I chair the panel discussion; a fist of nerves, dried river mud splashed around the heels of my boots.

The next morning, I avoid the river path and walk the main road to the station. The noise of cars rushing over wet tarmac, tyre press like bubble wrap, twists my stomach muscles up. In the stubborn gloom, Mars is a bright rose freckle, hovering west towards the river. I realise that I've never seen it there before: only east, at night, pointed out in the wide strip of universe above our narrow street.

In December, the full moon cuts a bright circle into the diluted image of the train's interior. It ignites the wisping clouds scraped across it. Streetlights zip past, piercing the image, too, like watery shooting stars. I watch my mouth curve into a flickering smile.

Back in York, though it's been dark for hours, the river path is busy with dogs circling each other's scent and owners rubbing palms while they talk. The water is invisible, signalled only by the orange light slithering among its ripples. The air is still and cold and clear. From the bottom of our street, I spot the moon again.

For the first time in eight years, I notice that I am coming home to the same house I was coming home to twelve months ago.

I slow my pace, glancing up again, and then again, to enjoy this radiance hanging right above the pavement. The light reflecting from our moon's surface is just a little too bright to rest my eyes upon.

I pass new wreaths hung on various front doors. I cross the street and swing my bag onto one shoulder so that I can search for my key. The yellow lamp is lit in the front room. I take one more look at the moon, and step inside.

ST LAWRENCE RIVER, QUEBEC CITY.

4.50 P.M.

Down on the harbourside, the colours are like sugar paper – a chalk pastel rainbow fading blue, to yellow, to pink and down into the dusty purple hills on the horizon. The whole thing is repeated in the water.

The river is flat and still like oil, snow-crusted ice sitting on its surface. The broken slabs interrupt the reflection, clustered here and there, scrunched and slushy where the parting boats have made room for more sky.

The air is bristling, alive with cold. You are aware of your eyes widening in wonder at this candyfloss view, exposing just a fraction more of your warm body to its bite. You are standing close to the edge, up on the concrete ribbon, boots planted in the frosted powder. You turn to look behind. Snow is piled up in dry heaps, obscuring the base of the hillside. And up, right up above the frozen trees, reach the fairy-tale turrets of the Château Frontenac. The whole thing seems imaginary. Like it's been dreamt into a watercolour painting.

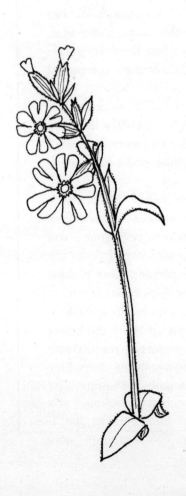

NEW YEAR'S DAY

'We're on the edge of the weather,' he says.

And he's right: the sky is split right down the middle, and we seem to be standing directly under its seam. Dark, pinkish grey on one side, clean blue on the other.

I nod. 'It's winter on the left, and summer on the right.'

But the sea, roiling underneath, is full-furious with winter energy. It is cut-glass green, pale from aeration, whipped up and fizzing with oxygen. We are halfway down our scramble and have stopped to watch a particularly fierce wave meet the cliffs. It sends a plume of spray into the air, which falls back in the wind and is embraced by the next, even bigger assault. We observe, mesmerised for a while, and then just as I'm wondering if we'll even venture down to the lower level today, Dad continues on.

As I follow, carefully, the muscle memory of this route down the rocks, my eyes habitually scan the nooks and creases for bullets. My subconscious is looking for a slim glimpse of oxidised turquoise, a smooth caplet, half buried in the grit of an ancient groove. This section of coastline is owned by the Ministry of Defence, and my older siblings and I treasure-hunted here competitively as children, rejecting splays of metal which, though also weathered-bright, had been denigrated to shrapnel by the limestone.

I have often wondered how many spent bullets must lie rusting out there, in the sand down under the waves.

The last part of the descent has changed since I was a teenager. A few years ago, a section of the rock wall split, falling away just a little, leaving a narrow chimney for us to shimmy down. Dad goes down first, and I think that the slice looks a fraction further away from the wall than it did last time. The open cut is coppery and rough, un-weathered by the waves that the outer rock has seen. The wound sparkles with minerals that, until recently, had not seen sunlight for…how long? Millennia? My palms and toes push hard against either side, until one boot finds the familiar boulder at the bottom. I scrape my right raincoat sleeve and then drop down to the next plateau.

This level is grid-lined and puddled with salt water. I keep a wary eye on the waves coming in. We haven't seen any reach this high, but people talk about rogue waves, and the crag-pools seem to imply that we're not guaranteed a dry time here.

I can think of only one occasion – when I was about sixteen – that we didn't dare to come down to this lower level. The wind had reached about fifty miles per hour back at the house, whistling up and around its pebble-dash walls. Dad and I climbed into the campervan and drove to the coast, desperate to see how strong the gale was there. In the carpark on the cliff, we parked and sat for a while in the front seats while the high-topped van rocked on its suspension. A seagull hugged the ground, legs folded under, in the middle of the empty clearing, unable to open its wings. We decided to manoeuvre the van around, pointing its nose into the gale, realising that there was a very real possibility it might turn over if we left it sidelong. Like a small boat facing the roll and swell of shore-bound waves.

Eventually we fastened every zip and popper of our coats and wrestled the doors open. The wind was breath-*stealing*. I had never felt anything like it. Knowing that the force was all rushing inland – that we were not quite in danger of being flung off the cliffs and out to sea – we made our way towards the usual edge. What is normally a few minutes' stride across sea-tough grass seemed to take an hour. Walking against the elements, every step was a battle. I felt like a figure in a painting, a smudge of limbs slanted in towards the horizon.

Dad was further ahead, but we couldn't call to each other – couldn't hear a thing except the roar of air over Gore-Tex. When he tells the story, he says he looked around to check I was still behind him, and that when he looked again a minute later, just before going over the first rocky edge, I was gone.

In fact, I was about thirty yards further back: face down and body flat to the ground.

My memory is clear: labouring towards the sea, I had turned my face back inland for a breath of respite. At the same moment, a particularly strong gust had hit my back, like a shove between the shoulder blades, and my unsteady feet obeyed. I was pushed along, back towards the van, until I realised that the momentum had become faster than I could run, and that I wasn't in control. I made a quick decision to take my legs out of the equation and hit the ground.

Dad arrived to find me flat out and laughing down among the tussocks. We tried again and ventured over the first edge together. Then we found the nearest nook – a wall of immovable rock to press ourselves against – and settled in to watch the storm. A Turner sea; a chaos of uncontainable energy. They reckon the gale force reached almost one hundred miles per hour on the range that day.

Today, the water writhes and tumbles, heaving its restless weight against the same tall cliffs. It throws its frosted edges up, crystal branches reaching into the yellow light, then caught again by the water's push and pull. The campaign grows frenzied, building with each wave in its cycle. A geyser of foam blasts up the rock face. The low sun catches all the cells in its body, every pin-prick bubble of its mass, lighting it bright white against the dark grey cliff behind.

I notice Dad turn to consider the ledge behind us. It's a jagged lip which traverses the crook of a deep gash in the coastline. Rocks and water churn way down below. We often take this route around to the wider plateau stretching out under the cliffs to our left. There we have spent plenty of calm summer evenings, scrutinising the seams in the rock, flexing fingers, finding quiet routes up the vertical sea wall. Or sat close to the water, watching gannets skim the horizon, or perhaps a whiskered face blink back at us from the blue.

He turns away, but then walks two paces further out on the peninsular we're standing on. This pot-holed level reaches a crooked wrist out, just twenty feet or so, among the waves. On its end balances a boulder about the size of a round hay bale after harvest: a black silhouette perched firmly on its pedestal.

Usually, we go right to the end and lean on this boulder, the Atlantic sloshing on three sides. When I was nineteen, I pressed my back against the cold weight of it and filled my lungs with the air rushing up off the ocean. My silly broken heart was sore under my ribs, and my friends waited impatiently on the sheep-shorn grass above.

I often try to imagine this boulder's journey to the end of its peninsular. I wonder how long it has been here, and, with a little sadness, when it will finally complete its descent.

The coast rumbles. Thunder that somehow resonates deep down below our feet and in our chests. Unseen cavities snort with the sudden compression of air. I imagine these cliffs as old and weary, enduring patiently what the sea cannot help but inflict. Brine drains from their cracks, streaming over barnacles. Water sucks back, gathers weakly, and collapses low against the rocks again with none of its previous conviction. That last one must have been number eleven: the cycle starts again.

It took far too many years for me to reflect on the wild quality of much of our coastline and realise that it is this unrelenting conflict which causes it. Cliffs like these are warzones, our island's bones faced bare to the power of the sea. They are in a constant state of change – and change as we humans know it: the daily drag of the inevitable tides, restless weather, rolling seasons. The persistent – the irreversible – nag of erosion. The space between high-tide and low is special, never wet or dry or safe for long, protected by its changeability and, under most laws, not even stamped with ownership.

In this busy and crowded country, you can stand on a gnarl of rock, the ocean licking at your feet, and know with certainty that it would be here even if you weren't. Even if no human foot had ever pressed the Earth, this lump of mineral would exist exactly as it is now.

There's not much we can do with a battlefield like this one. It makes our bricks and walls and tarmac seem like tinsel. It rejects our tampering ways. It carries on: scouring the raw edge of the land, grinding, showcasing its layers of deep time.

Nearby there are scrunched and slanting stripes – visible from the vantage point beside the lonely boulder – which let us see 345 million years of different lands and atmospheres all at once. I've known the contours of those cliffs for longer than my pen recalls, but I'd never stopped to think how honest they were; how much they told.

'We're not going round there today,' I say to Dad. I can tell that the brief lull in energy below us has turned his thoughts back to the traverse. He's tempted by the Russian roulette of sea spray; I'm thinking of the possibility of a rogue wave dragging us down into the churn.

I'm watching the lichen-green lift and fold. Foam laces the surface. Currents tug at the rest of the cliff beneath. I imagine myself in the water, measure my chances of getting out. I know that my eyes, even today, underestimate the strength in each collapse of water onto rock. I have played this episode many times before.

'Perhaps not today,' Dad says. The waves are gathering pace again, and we agree to wait for the next crescendo before heading back. The sea carries on its tireless heft against the blackened limestone walls and will continue until the watery sun sinks into night.

We turn to face our way back up, and a sea-froth firework erupts: it rises from the gulley beside us and drenches the ledge we would have been halfway across by now, had we decided to venture on. We laugh together, heads back and shoulders shrugged, then start our familiar ascent.

'I got soaked here once,' Dad says as he finds a foothold further up. 'Must have been the wind caught it. Nothing... then turned my back, and suddenly, a wall of spray.'

Back on top, we take the long curve back to the car, skirting around the edge of the cliffs, peering over at the white horses tossing below. The golden light has faded now, and the storm clouds seem to be scowling darker than before.

I linger for a moment, drinking deep the air: the weather, the seething water and the prickling wind.

AUTHOR'S NOTES

A note on places

When I made most of the memories in this book, I knew certain places by their English names – names more familiar to me and I imagine to most readers. Since then, those places have been rightly returned to their native Welsh names, and so here I have referred to them accordingly. Cymraeg is a language full of story – and I'm not sure the convenience of visiting tongues is a good enough reason to let those stories disappear.

A note on people

Non-fiction involves real people – but there's still some creative licence. I've changed a couple of names where I felt it was right to do so, and not all speech is quoted word for word. These are stories told in my own way – and while memory cannot always be relied upon, it is truth, nonetheless.

ACKNOWLEDGEMENTS

This is my first published book, so I'm afraid I'm going all out on these.

Let's start from the top: thank you, Mum and Dad. You are wonderful, and I owe most things, ultimately, to you. Thanks as well to my brilliant big siblings – for what I fondly refer to as 'character building'. And to Imogen, who's been right there since before we could do up our own coat zips.

The teachers: Miss Thomas, who told me with such certainty in year 8 that I was *a writer*. Sam at Durham, who reminded me that I still wanted to be just that. My brilliant teachers at Manchester, especially Horatio, who introduced me to the real joy of the essay, and Jeanette, who kept us all going in a hell or high water. And Jane, who taught me how to tap dance.

My writing buddies: you know who you are. George you are such a constant. And Rozie, you have helped me more than I think you know, and I admire you so.

Thanks also to the lovely authors who have supported me and *Seaglass* with their time and words – it's meant a lot.

Acknowledgements

And to all my endlessly enthusiastic friends and family – on both sides of the Atlantic!

To everyone at New Writing North: the best colleagues I might ever have! All those train commutes and late nights writing – they were so worth it to be able to work with you all. And to Claire and Carol for the perfectly-timed gift of a week in Gordon's magic little cottage.

Calon: a small and mighty team, who are doing brilliant work. Thanks, Amy, for sending the email that started it all, and Abbie, for taking the reins with such care. Thanks as well to Gwen and the *New Welsh Review* for choosing 'Return to Water', way back when.

And, of course, to Andrew. Since that evening when I stood in your messy student kitchen and told you I was going to write, you've taken those words as fact. Thank you, for treating my eyelash-dreams with the utmost seriousness. And for everything else, too.